D1521479

MAKERS
of the
MUSLIM
WORLD

Nazira Zeineddine

TITLES IN THE MAKERS OF
THE MUSLIM WORLD SERIES

Series Editor: Patricia Crone,
Institute for Advanced Study, Princeton

Abd al-Ghani al-Nabulusi, Samer Akkach
'Abd al-Malik, Chase F. Robinson
Abd al-Rahman III, Maribel Fierro
Abu Nuwas, Philip Kennedy
Ahmad al-Mansur, Mercedes García-Arenal
Ahmad ibn Hanbal, Christopher Melchert
Ahmad Riza Khan Barelwi, Usha Sanyal
Akbar, André Wink
Al-Ma'mun, Michael Cooperson
Al-Mutanabbi, Margaret Larkin
Amir Khusraw, Sunil Sharma
Ashraf 'Ali Thanawi, Muhammad Qasim Zaman
Chinggis Khan, Michal Biran
El Hajj Beshir Agha, Jane Hathaway
Fazlallah Astarabadi and the Hurufis, Shazad Bashir
Ghazali, Eric Ormsby
Hasan al-Banna, Gudrun Krämer
Husain Ahmad Madani, Barbara Metcalf
Ibn 'Arabi, William C. Chittick
Ibn Fudi, Ahmad Dallal
Ikhwan al-Safa, Godefroid de Callatay
Karim Khan Zand, John R. Perry
Mehmed Ali, Khaled Fahmy
Mu'awiya ibn abi Sufyan, R. Stephen Humphreys
Muhammad Abduh, Mark Sedgwick
Nasser, Joel Gordon
Sa'di, Homa Katouzian
Shaykh Mufid, Tamima Bayhom-Daou
Usama ibn Munqidh, Paul M. Cobb

For current information and details of other books in the
series, please visit www.oneworld-publications.com

MAKERS
of the
MUSLIM
WORLD

Nazira Zeineddine
A Pioneer Of
Islamic Feminism

miriam cooke

ONEWORLD
OXFORD

NAZIRA ZEINEDDINE

A Oneworld Book
Published by Oneworld Publications 2010

ISBN 978–1–85168–769–5

Typeset by Jayvee, Trivandrum, India
Printed and bound in India by Imprint Digital

Oneworld Publications
UK: 185 Banbury Road, Oxford, OX2 7AR, England
USA: 38 Greene Street, 4th Floor, New York, NY 10013, USA

CONTENTS

Illustrations vi
Maps viii
Preface xi
Acknowledgements xviii

PART I

1 **EARLY ARAB FEMINISMS** 3
2 **THE TWILIGHT OF THE OTTOMANS** 13
3 **ISLAMIC LESSONS** 29
4 **RELIGIOUS INTERLOCUTORS** 39
5 **THE BOOK** 51
6 **"THE GIRL" WRITES BACK** 69
7 **WHAT WENT WRONG?** 87

PART II

8 **MARRIAGE** 103
9 **THE AFTERLIFE OF A WRITER** 119
   CONCLUSION 129

Glossary 133
Works Cited 135
Index 139

ILLUSTRATIONS

Portrait of Nazira Zeineddine ix

PART I

The Zeineddine Mansion in Ayn Qani xii
The al-Halabi Mansion in Baaqline xiii
Charles de Gaulle's residence 1923–1932 xiv
Zeineddine Pasha Hasan al-Khatib (courtesy of Said
    Zeineddine) 14
Said Bey Zeineddine (courtesy of Said Zeineddine) 15
Said and Hala (courtesy of Said Zeineddine) 16
Ayn Qani Terrace 22
Photograph of Nazira and Asmahan (courtesy of Said
    Zeineddine) 26
Nazira outside Karakol Druze house (courtesy of Said
    Zeineddine) 29
Nazira and Munira in Beirut 1920 (courtesy of Said
    Zeineddine) 30
Druze women 56
Letter from Syrian prime pinister, Taj al-Din
    al-Hasani 61
Poem from King Fu'ad, "The Voice of Truth"
    (courtesy of Said Zeineddine) 65
Review of The Girl and the Shaykhs 78

PART II

Nazira with Arij (courtesy of Said Zeineddine) 110
Nazira with her nephew Said (courtesy of Said
    Zeineddine) 117
Druze tomb in Baaqline 127

MAPS

1. Map of Ayn Qani Region 17

2. Map showing Beirut and Ayn Qani Region 20

Portrait of Nazira Zeineddine by her son Arij al-Halabi

PREFACE

In late 1928 the Thabits threw a party to celebrate the publication of a book about women and Islam. The rich and famous of Lebanon and Syria, including even the Syrian prime minister, Taj al-Din al-Hasani, were in attendance. The prime minister arrived late, but as far as the editor of *The Lost Journalist* was concerned, "the absence of the sun in the sky did not eclipse the brilliant light of the suns that filled the sumptuous halls of the Thabit palace, foremost among them Miss Nazira Zeineddine, author of *Unveiling and Veiling*. She was 'la femme du jour'" (*The Girl and the Shaykhs (Al-fatat wa al-shuyukh)*, p. 23).

Nazira Zeineddine was a Druze woman from Lebanon who single-handedly took on the Islamic authorities of her day. Heedless of their power, she wrote two long books in defense of Muslim women's rights. Her carefully crafted polemic against the face veil, her passionate defense of women's intellectual equality with men, and her condemnation of institutionalized misogyny among men of religion caused a furor. Within five years, however, the writer and her books slipped between the lines of history. The clerics had won.

In *Opening the Gates. A Century of Arab Feminist Writing,* an anthology Margot Badran and I published in 1990, we included a snippet from *Unveiling and Veiling*. Readers were intrigued by this text which anticipated the *fin de siècle* Islamic feminist movement by over sixty years. Who was this Nazira Zeineddine? What shot her into the stratosphere of international attention? How was it that such a luminary should shine so briefly and then be extinguished so completely? We didn't know. Then in 1998, Syrian scholar and politician Bouthaina Shaaban blew the dust off the two books and reprinted them. The arguments of *Unveiling and Veiling* and *The Girl and the Shaykhs* were as fresh and relevant as they had been in 1928 and 1929. But the story of her life remained unknown.

For years, the only biographical information I could find were passing references to her education scattered in her two books. Then, in the summer of 2007, Lebanese political scientist Aida al-Jawhari published *Ramziyat al-hijab: mafahim wa dalalat* (Symbolism of the Veil: Concepts and Meanings), an analysis of both books. It included a six-page biography of Nazira's father Said Bey Zeineddine, a lawyer who had trained in Istanbul at the end of the nineteenth century. He had worked in several Ottoman cities in today's Turkey and Syria and was then appointed the first president of the court of appeals in Beirut.

With this information in hand, I traveled to Kozan, Adana, Istanbul, and Edirne Province in Turkey where Nazira's father had held various posts. I found nothing. In the summer of 2008, the centenary of Nazira's birth, I flew to Lebanon, and pieces of the puzzle

The Zeineddine Mansion in Ayn Qani

The al-Halabi Mansion in Baaqline

tumbled into place. I learned that Nazira was born in Istanbul and that her childhood home was a three-hundred-year-old mansion in Ayn Qani, a tiny village perched high in the Druze Mountains of the Chouf.

From Ayn Qani I drove the ten miles to Baaqline, where her husband's mansion is now a college for Druze students. In the sixteenth century, the Druze Prince Fakhruddin had ruled the region from Baaqline.

I discovered that she had had a sister and two brothers, and had married and had three sons. I met some of the surviving members of her family. Her youngest brother's only son, Said Zeineddine, gave me photographs and letters, and a book hot off the press. It was *Nazira Zeineddine: Pioneer of Women's Liberation* by Nabil Bu Matar, his Arabic teacher at the Chouf National College in Baaqline. During Teacher's Day in 1981, Said had given Bu Matar his aunt's two books. A few years later, while Said was studying in Egypt he learned that the books had inspired his teacher to write a thesis. However, Bu Matar died in 1995 before finishing the book. It took thirteen more years for his wife Hayat to complete the project, and the book was published in August 2008, a few days before my arrival. In November, I traveled to Kuwait to interview Said at greater length.

I spent time with Samia Saab, daughter of Nazira's cousin, Najla Saab (1908–1971) with whom Nazira spent the World War I years in Ayn Qani. Samia drove me to Karakol Druze where Nazira had grown up. The Zeineddine house had been next to the building where Charles de Gaulle had stayed between 1929 and 1932, during his first tour of duty in the Mandate army. We found the building, with a sign recording de Gaulle's stay, but next to it was a parking lot. The house had been torn down years earlier.

Next, we went to her sister Nabila whose apartment overlooks the heavily guarded complex of the Shiite Amal leader Nabih Berri. Together they reminisced about life with Nazira's father who had

Charles de Gaulle's residence 1923–1932

been like a grandfather to them. They called him Jiddu, an Arabic term of endearment for grandfather.

I met both of Nazira's surviving sons, Arij and Nabil. I spent an afternoon with Arij who happened to be in Beirut when I was there, and, in the spring of 2009, I traveled to Monticagnalia in Sardinia to interview Nabil.

It was only after I met her family that I gradually began to recognize the "I" in the exegetical texts. I started to make sense of the passion in what I had expected to be dry and dusty exegesis; a dryness and dustiness I had been surprised not to find in *Al-sufur wa al-hijab* and *Al-fatat wa al-shuyukh*. Autobiography can be inadvertent, random facts hidden in the interstices of fiction but also of scholarship. A reflexive gesture, autobiographical tidbits can open up the career of someone who had not thought to write her life. This is true of Nazira Zeineddine whose biography I have written without benefit of any intentional biographical writing on her part. How could I tell the story of the missing decades between the publication of two books in the late 1920s and her death in 1976?

The places she had inhabited, the things she had used, and the family photographs revealed biographical resonances in the religious polemic. I recognized the importance of what I had previously considered to be a grammatical quirk: the use of the second person masculine singular and plural that ran through both books. The two Islamic feminist treatises became complex texts that interwove hermeneutics and autobiographical fragments.

It was the enmeshing of these fragments in the larger texts that told the story of a girl constructing her self in the process of challenging the shaykhs. These exegetical texts started to tell her life story between isolation in a palace in a Druze village tucked in the highest folds of the Chouf mountains and integration into the elite cosmopolitan and multi-confessional community of late 1920s Beirut. *Tafsir* (commentary) served as a veil over a life narrative that was told in a tone that would have been considered inappropriate in polite society. Writing the biography was not just a matter of framing the texts in the place and time in which they were produced. It compelled a re-reading, even a new reading of the two books and then weaving them into the fabric of her life and her time. Each became necessary to the other as the one undid and rewove the design.

After trips to Turkey, Lebanon, Kuwait, and Italy, and interviewing friends and family, I had learned many facts about Nazira's life, but a mystery lingered: why had she stopped writing?

In telling her life, I have tried to fill in the missing decades between the publication of her two books in the late 1920s and her death in 1976. I have relied on several sources: autobiographical information that Nazira included in her books, articles, and letters; the stories acquaintances related to me; the two recently published books; and the information I gathered from things like family furniture and photographs. I have traveled to the places she inhabited to get some sense of her homes and the mood of her era. When I quote conversations I may have taken passages from one of her books that were so powerful and vivid they read like direct speech, or I have used stories her relatives narrated to construct a dramatic exchange.

The challenge facing biographers is how to weave the strands of a person's life into the larger political and historical tapestry of their time. Even when they have more facts than I was able to uncover, biographers must imagine connections between moments that have shaped the person's life. For Graham McCann, the biographer "invents her form and, through language directs the reader's impressions, images, and interpretation of the subject ... No biographer merely records a life; every biographer, no matter how objective she declares herself, interprets a life" (McCann 1991, p. 327). And this is what I have tried to do in writing the biography of a woman over whose adult life a curtain has fallen.

Nazira's fierce defense of women's rights to make their own choices about their lives and their bodies has acquired a renewed resonance. In the era of Islamist activism that gained ground in the 1980s, after the Islamic Revolution succeeded in Iran and inspired others, Muslim women's rights have been jeopardized and women are retaliating. I have had my own experiences of how vital and controversial Nazira's writing remains.

During that visit to Lebanon in the summer of 2008, a friend emailed me, warning that "to mention Nazira or to focus on her as a liberated woman is impossible nowadays. It will be harmful to you and to us. Nazira could easily be taken as another Salman Rushdie. It is not the right time for it."

A few months later, just before delivering a talk about Nazira at a Gulf university, I was asked to change my topic. My host cautioned that it would be dangerous for me and also for the administration if I were to be critical of veiling. While women were engaged in a struggle with conservative shaykhs over the appropriateness of the face veil, an American woman should not interfere. I protested that the opinions I was going to present were not my own but those of a Lebanese woman who had written eighty years earlier. No, the audience would think I was hiding behind this woman's words. Half of my talk was cut. I was told to emphasize the difference between the face veil, or the *niqab*, of the 1920s that had been a tool of the state disabling women's education and participation in the public sphere, and the veil of 2008 that was a matter of personal choice, and no longer an instrument of oppression and ignorance. My counselor was a sixty-year-old professor, who would shudder at the thought of covering her hair, let alone her face. She was genuinely worried about my safety. And I, less courageous than Nazira, caved in to pressure, agreed to the deletions, and gave a very short talk. The audience was perplexed: what was so controversial about Nazira Zeineddine?

ACKNOWLEDGEMENTS

M any people have helped me in my search for Nazira Zeineddine and I am very grateful to all of them. In Turkey local historians, especially Nazif Karacam in Kirklareli, gave me a sense of their country before the founding of the republic in 1924. In Antakya, where I went because I thought Nazira had referred to this ancient city with special interest, Serra and Abdullah Sehoğlu, owners of the Savon Hotel, were unstinting in their generosity as they threw themselves and their friends into my search for any trace of the Zeineddines.

I am indebted to many in Lebanon. First of all, my dear friend the Sufi poet Huda Naamani provided me with the first piece of the puzzle of Nazira's life when she insisted that I return to Lebanon to look for clues. She threw a party for me on my arrival and invited Aida al-Jawhari. Aida handed me several more pieces that filled out gaps in the family history and she drove me into the Chouf Mountains to visit Nazira's homes. Linda and Fawzi Jumblat from Ayn Qani told me about Nazira's generosity and respect for everyone regardless of status.

The picture came into sharp focus thanks to help I received from family members Nina al-Atrash, Samia and Nabila Saab, and especially Nazira's nephew, Said Zeineddine, and her sons Arij and Nabil. All of them gave generously of their time and provided me with any information I needed. I spent an afternoon with Arij, an interior designer and artist, who returns every summer to check on the Baaqline house. Surrounded by his parents' furniture in his Khalde apartment, he knows exactly where each item had been in the Beirut or Baaqline residence and who had used what, where, and when. But the only memory he has of his mother is the day in 1957 shortly before his fourteenth birthday when Beirut was shaken by an earthquake. Nabil was very generous to me when I spent a week in Sardinia in the summer of 2009. Also an architect, he was quite unlike his brother. He had kept nothing from his childhood and adolescence; he had thrown out every letter and photograph that tied him to his past. Once, he had tried to read one of his mother's books but he had given up after a few pages of difficult Arabic. But his sentimental attachment to his mother was immense, and his vivid memories of his childhood and teenage years were invaluable in helping me tie together many of the loose ends that had started to become tangled in my mind.

In America also, many have helped me, especially the Middle East reading group from Duke University and the University of North Carolina in Chapel Hill, and the Women's Autobiographies in Islamic Societies network meeting in Austin, Texas, in January 2010.

I want to thank Ellen McLarney who gave me excellent feedback on an early version. My special thanks go to my student Dania Toth who was an astute reader and a remarkable editor. As always, my best critic, friend, and inspiration is my partner forever Bruce Lawrence.

PART I

EARLY ARAB FEMINISMS

She couldn't stop writing.

For weeks, she had woken up early and gone right back to where she had left off the night before.

"So, how's it coming along?"

"I'm almost there ...," she beamed with pleasure at her father's interest.

She wrote until her hand hurt. The book tyrannized every moment of her life. She was still in disbelief that the previous summer shaykhs in Damascus had managed to persuade the government to impose the face veil on all Muslim women when they left their homes.

"How dare you take upon yourselves what God did not even enjoin on his Prophet Muhammad?" she muttered as she wrote, "How do you presume to compel the people to do what you want? Where did you get the idea that you have the right to be our guardians?" (*Unveiling and Veiling*, pp. 48–49)

On 18 March 1928 she crossed the last t of *Unveiling and Veiling*. She could not have anticipated the reactions to her book but she knew that writing it was the imperative of the moment.

To veil or not to veil? For over fifty years discussion and debate about the face veil had raged in the Muslim Arab world. In 1870 Butrus al-Bustani (1819–1883) founded the progressive pro-women's rights paper, *Al-Jinan*. The first publication to circulate throughout Syria,

Iraq, and Egypt, it had a large female readership due to its many articles on women's equality and their right to be educated. Writers referred to Western feminist thinkers like John Stuart Mill, Mary Wollstonecraft, and Elizabeth Cady Stanton. Their writings did not reflect the anxiety characteristic of later works that avoided mention of Western intellectual models lest their authors be accused of supporting European designs on the region (Zachs & Halevi 2009, pp. 618–623).

During the nineteenth century, the British and French had been displacing the Ottoman Turks who had ruled over much of the Arab world for five hundred years. World War I turned the twilight of the mighty Ottoman Empire into night, and the British and the French took over, establishing educational and political institutions in countries on the eastern and southern shores of the Mediterranean. Their presence helped American missionary enterprises to found the Protestant academies in Lebanon and Egypt that would later be called the American University in Beirut and the American University of Cairo. The norms and values of the European Enlightenment with its emphasis on reason, freedom, and equality were spreading, and challenging the worldview of conservative Muslims. Some welcomed the challenge, but many did not, and the face veil became an axis around which polemics revolved.

In European eyes, the face veil was emblematic of the "quintessential otherness and inferiority of Islam ... [and] the oppression of women" (Ahmed 1992, pp. 149, 153). It was deemed to be the major obstacle to modernizing and civilizing Muslim societies. Dividing these communities between their barbaric men and their civilizeable women, the colonizers focused their energies on saving women from their men by unveiling them and calling for their education and greater visibility in society.

Although many Muslims mistrusted the European obsession with the veil, some agreed that it constituted an obstacle to modernization. Few were more forthright in their condemnation of the face veil than the Egyptian aristocrat Aisha al-Taimuriya (1840–1902). In the introduction to her 1888 novel, *The Results of Circumstances in Words and Deeds*, she praised her father for his support of her education but lamented the state of society:

> So I studied the histories to the best of my ability, and to the extent that my dull mind could understand them – since it was not possible for me to enter the assemblages of the learned scholars and since the sessions of the erudite were not expanded to include me. How my chest was inflamed with the fire of longing to enter the paradise of their gatherings! How my eyelids overflowed with tears because I was deprived of harvesting the fruits of their beneficial learning! What hindered me from realizing this hope was the tent-like screen of an all-enveloping wrap.

In an 1889 article published in *Al-Adab* newspaper, she reiterated her frustration:

> Perhaps I am not qualified to speak in this sphere, and I admit to my limited powers of grasping the subject at hand—for I am secluded by the tent of an enveloping wrap. Yet, across its borders, I perceive that programs of education are treasure chests, and I see that the paths of refinement hold, at their ends, the keys to every gem that lies hidden.
> (Badran & cooke 1990, pp. 127, 129)

She is explicit about the fact that the face veil, or wrap, blocks understanding. However, she is just as clear about another fact, and that is that veiled women may remain aware of the possibility of understanding, but only once they have been freed of the wrap.

Not only for Aisha al-Taimuriya, but also for other women activists, education was the key to progress and it had to be made available to women. So did work. In 1891 Lebanese encyclopedist Zaynab Fawwaz drew attention to the progress of the West because women can "compete with the men and participate equally with them in work" (Badran & cooke 1990, p. 223).

In 1899, the French-educated Egyptian judge, Qasim Amin, argued that true Islam had lost its moorings and was shrouded in innovations that discriminated against women. Like Aisha al-Taimuriya, Amin argued that the face veil hindered access to education, public goods, and happiness in a companionate marriage.

Anticipating later arguments, he declared that the veil was not Islamic but rather a custom that belonged to another era. Many trace the visibility of what came to be called the Woman Question to the 1899 publication of Amin's *Liberation of Women*. This Sharia-based book indicted Muslim societies and their shaykhs who misinterpreted the Qur'an and the Sunna in such a way as to deprive women of their God-given rights. Some criticized the judge for collaborating with the British occupiers, especially Lord Cromer, who had been calling for the same reforms as part of their "civilizing mission," the term many adopted for the colonizing project (Ahmed 1992, p.159). A year later, Amin published a rejoinder in a book he titled *The New Woman*. Without naming his opponents, he tried to discredit their critiques. Amin dedicated this book, emblematic of the search for the New Woman, to Sa'd Zaghlul, a staunch supporter of women who would later lead the Egyptian nationalist movement.

They may not have received the kind of attention lavished on Qasim Amin, but Arab women were becoming actively involved in the debates about women's rights and roles in society. At the end of the nineteenth century, they began to establish their own journals and magazines that built on such reformist arguments. The very first was Hind Nawfal's *Al-Fatat* (1892). By the outbreak of World War I there were almost thirty journals owned, edited, and published by women in Cairo, Beirut, Damascus, and Baghdad. These publications included, in Egypt, Alexandra Afernuh's *Anis al-Jalis* (1898), Saadiya Saad al-Din's *Shajarat al-Durr* (1901), and Labiba Hashim's *Fatat al-Sharq* (1906); and in Lebanon, Salima Abu Rashid's *Fatat Lubnan* (1914). After World War I new journals and newspapers appeared, including Afifa Saab's *Al-Khidr* (1919) and Julia Tu'ma Dimashqiya's three papers, *Samir al-Sighar* (1920), *Al-Mar'a al-Jadida* (1921), and *Al-Nadim* (1926), and Marie Yani 'Atallah's *Minerva* (1923).

Shaaban writes that most authors "stressed the necessity to benefit from the experiences of other women without losing sight of Arab history, culture, and religion" (Shaaban 1993, pp. 76–77). The challenge they faced was how to balance their praise of women's achievements in European societies with a robust defense of their own cultures' norms and values.

A noteworthy feature of many of these papers was the inclusion of biographies of famous women in the East and West whose lives exemplified women's historically effective participation at all levels of society. The 1892 inaugural issue of *Al-Fatat* highlighted Joan of Arc as a model for contemporary women. In her analysis of the role of biography in Egyptian gender politics, Marilyn Booth writes: "for writers in Egypt to explain Jeanne's [Joan] mission as a divine one suited a milieu in which obedience was unquestioningly a matter of submission to divine law. Of even greater salience was the notion of religiosity as providing an unassailable sanction and source of energy for nationalist action" (Booth 2001, p. 250). Joan of Arc became a prototype for women who found empowerment through commitment to God. How could a father, husband, or brother assert control over the woman who had been selected for a higher calling?

While all insisted on the value to society of educated women, some argued that this education was not so much for the sake of the women but for their sons, the next generation of male leaders. Mention of women's rights and activism in Europe or in America was carefully calibrated lest advocacy of women's roles in the public sphere be labeled pro-Western and therefore unpatriotic. Arguments for women's rights and unveiling were hedged with qualifications including the claim that references to progressive Western norms were not a call to copy but only to learn. In 1910, Egyptian Bahithat al-Badiya cautioned that appreciation did not mean unthinking emulation: "I am the first to respect among them those who deserve respect, but respect for others should not make us overlook the good of the nation" (Badran & cooke 1990, p. 236). Arab women were tiptoeing on to the stage of regional history.

In 1919, a women's demonstration in Cairo hit the headlines. They were protesting against the British exclusion of Sa'd Zaghlul and his *wafd* (delegation) from the Versailles Peace Conference where the Arab world was to be carved up between European spheres of control. When Zaghlul was deported, demonstrations were held in

Egyptian towns, and the Wafd Party came into existence. Some of the demonstrators were wives of prominent men and their leader was Sa'd's wife, Safiyya Zaghlul. During her husband's exile, Safiyya promoted his message that women should unveil, and she held meetings in their home, the so-called "House of the Nation." Less than a year after the end of World War I, Egyptian women were acknowledged to be important to the success of the anti-colonial struggle (Baron 2005, pp. 135–161).

On his return from exile Zaghlul met with a group of women. Quoting Mayy Ziyada (1886–1941), the Palestinian-Lebanese woman whose salon hosted the Cairo literati every Tuesday evening, Nazira wrote that he warned the women he was about to address that he would not speak unless each uncovered her face. When he noticed that one woman remained veiled, he removed the cloth to the sound of applause and laughter. That for Nazira was the moment that launched the movement for the liberation of women. It was also an exemplary event for her: eight years later, when she was invited to talk to the Arab Literary Association, one of her conditions was that the women in the audience should not be veiled (*Unveiling and Veiling*, p. 142).

After 1919, Egyptian women activists no longer discussed issues of common concern in closed meetings but in clubs and associations. These "Mothers of the Nation" demanded attention to women's roles in the political arena, advocated reforms in both religious and civil laws, and campaigned for women's rights to education and suffrage. They anticipated the New Woman who was unveiled, educated, and happy in her bourgeois family with a loving husband by her side. When this loving husband died, as did Safiyya's in 1927, the wife might continue the fight for women's rights that were often conflated with the rights of the nation.

To counter this secularized image of the New Woman, the Muslim activist Labiba Ahmad introduced the "New Islamic Woman" who took part in society even if behind the veil (Baron 2005, p. 190). In 1923, her paper *Al-Nahda al-Nisa'iya* (Women's Awakening) took the lead in promoting the image of a modern, pious Muslim woman.

Women were revealing the patriarchal assumptions at the core of nationalist and reform movements whether European and secular or indigenous and Islamic.

Concerned not to raise anxiety about their demands for greater equality and visibility, some Muslim feminists used family-oriented and socially conservative language. Far from derailing moral norms, reform in women's rights, they argued, would enhance these norms and contribute to economic and political progress. In 1920, Nabawiya Musa wrote that professional work for women did not interfere with domestic duties, and she mentioned European models: "This is clear in England, Switzerland, Germany, and in other countries where the woman works until she marries and then she stays at home becoming a disciplined and well-organized mother who takes care of her children and [is] a good companion to her husband" (Badran & cooke 1990, p. 269). From this perspective, Western women do not pose a threat to Islam because they adhere to Muslim norms.

The face veil played a pivotal role in the debate over Muslim women's rights, and elite women fought to remove it. Throughout the 1920s, women were testing reactions to unveiling. In 1920, when Nazira was twelve, the Syrian Nazik al-`Abid Bayhum (1887–1960), editor of *Anwar al-Faiha'*, took off her veil during the battle against the French at Maysoloun. Three years later, Huda Shaarawi, president of the Egyptian Feminist Union, shocked the Muslim world when she stepped off a train in the Cairo railway station with her face uncovered. About the same time in Turkey, Ataturk, the father of the new republic, launched his secularism campaign with an attack on Islamic symbols, including turbans and veils. Nazira would later quote him: "My clear victory over the enemy is due half to the soldiers and half to the tearing of the veil from women's faces" (*The Girl and the Shaykhs*, p. 56).

Arab women were beginning to acknowledge each other's achievements in public. In her obituary for the Syrian Warda al-Yaziji, published in *Al-Muqtataf* in May 1924, Mayy Ziyada celebrated the life of a pioneer in the Arab women's literary awakening of the nineteenth century and announced women's responsibility to future generations "to uncover and register in existence the nature of the eastern woman, and to struggle thereafter to make sure that we help it to grow" (Badran & cooke 2004, pp. 240, 243). But as always with pro-women activities, the road ahead is not clear and the various struggles to uncover and register women's achievements is not always acknowledged. When Nazira died half a century later, her contributions to raising an Islamic feminist consciousness were not recognized; there was no Mayy to celebrate her contributions to the advancement of Muslim women's rights.

Whatever their approaches to women's public assertiveness, it appeared that a social revolution was under way. In cosmopolitan Beirut, a newly modernized port city with about 130,000 inhabitants, foreign women were changing the urban landscape. In 1915, the Turkish fighter and writer Khalida Adib Edivar walked around town with her face uncovered. Almost a decade before Ataturk launched his secularist campaign, Turkish women were looking to Europe for models. In the mid-1920s, French women accompanying the Mandate forces introduced Lebanese women to the latest fashions from Paris. Moreover, Egyptian women visitors to the region reinforced the belief of many that the veil was a thing of the past.

Syrian and Lebanese Muslim women began to appear in public with their faces uncovered, the upper classes wearing elegant turbans, flapper dresses, silk stockings, and high heels. Such were the provocations that drove some Syrian shaykhs in the summer of 1927 to call for mandatory veiling. Some zealots threw acid on women who left home unveiled.

Like Egyptian women eight years earlier, Syrian women took to the streets and Nazira Zeineddine to her pen. Citing scriptures and religious authorities on almost every page, she declared that the face veil was not Islamic. She wrote over four hundred pages about the harm to society of covering women's faces and argued for women's equality with men. Within a few months she had finished, and she published *Unveiling and Veiling: The Liberation of Women and Social Renewal in the Islamic World*. The second half of the title was a clear salute to Qasim Amin's 1899 book of the same title. Within a year she had received praise and censure in the Arab press but also in newspapers and magazines from South America, the United States, India, and Europe, and for months the letters poured in from Brazil, Argentina, Peru, Senegal, America, and various Arab countries. The book was a phenomenon.

THE TWILIGHT OF THE OTTOMANS

Unveiling and Veiling was so widely read and diversely received because it had the force of a religiously schooled, literarily accomplished writer. How did Nazira become so knowledgeable and authoritative in a field that was thought to be the preserve of men who had spent long years studying the basic texts of Islam? The answer is to be found in the story of her education and her relationship to her father.

An enlightened product of the decaying Ottoman system, Said Bey Zeineddine understood the importance of the Islamic education that had shaped him and that he then transmitted to his daughter (*The Girl and the Shaykhs*, pp. 115, 123, 124). Years of home schooling in the basics and not-so basics of Islam turned her into an Islamic scholar, and it is to him that she repeatedly declared her indebtedness for her ideas about women and Islam.

Said Bey was born in the Druze village of Ayn Qani in 1877. His father, Zeineddine Pasha Hasan al-Khatib, the feudal lord of the village, had fought in the 1860s Chouf battles against the Maronites. These battles marked the beginning of the end of Druze supremacy in the Chouf, because the growing influence of the French in the region favored the Maronites. But, like all ends, this one was not remarked at the time. The Druze ruling classes acted as though nothing had changed. They continued to send their sons to train as Islamic legal scholars whose authority mainstream Muslims did not question until decades later. It was only in 1924 with the abolition of the Ottoman Caliphate that the religious foundations of law and education were challenged. Legal education would no longer entail a lengthy study and thorough grasp of Islam. Lawyers would no longer be automatically considered Islamic authorities but only practitioners of the law of the land, whether it was secular or pertaining to a national or communal religion. The abolition of the Caliphate served to highlight religious differences in countries previously glossed as Muslim.

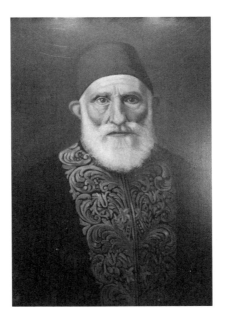

Zeineddine Pasha Hasan al-Khatib (courtesy of Said Zeineddine)

So it was that Zeineddine Pasha's sons, Muhammad and Said, attended the prestigious Madrasat al-Hikma and then the Ottoman Maktab secondary school in Beirut, where they learned Turkish in order to study law in Istanbul University. By 1896, when Said was only nineteen years old, he had earned his degree in the Ottoman capital, thus becoming not only an accomplished lawyer but also, and despite the fact that he was Druze, an acknowledged authority on the Qur'an and the Sunna.

His first assignment was to be public prosecutor in Anatolian Kozan. Seat of the magistrate's court and residence of the Grand Patriarch of Cilicia, with a population of about 3,500, Kozan was the first of his several postings to Ottoman provinces north of Beirut. Surrounded by Turkmen and Kurdish tribes, the town of Kozan is in the pine-covered Taurus Mountains north of Aleppo where tigers, panthers, wolves, bears, boars, and jackals were said to roam. Formerly Sis, the capital of the Cilician Kingdom of Armenia, its twelfth-century fortress controlled trade and communication between the coast and the interior. In 1896, there was just one road linking it to Adana on the Mediterranean (Cuinet 1891, pp. 87–93).

A year later, Said Bey moved northwest to multi-ethnic and multi-confessional Kirik Killiesi, today's Kirklareli, some two hundred

Said Bey Zeineddine (courtesy of Said Zeineddine)

kilometers from Istanbul and twenty from the Bulgarian border. At the time, nearby Edirne was the second capital of the Ottoman Empire. Edirne could not have changed much in the three hundred years that separated its heyday from the time Said Bey worked down the road in Kirik Killiesi. Situated in a rich agricultural region that boasted the best grapes and wine east of the Rhine, Byzantine Kirik Killiesi had fallen to the Ottomans in 1368. Today the fine city square, the Yayla Meidan, is a sad reminder of better days. The governor's mansion and municipal buildings where Said Bey had worked were burnt down during the 1920 struggle with the Greeks for control of Thrace.

Said Bey and Hala (courtesy of Said Zeineddine)

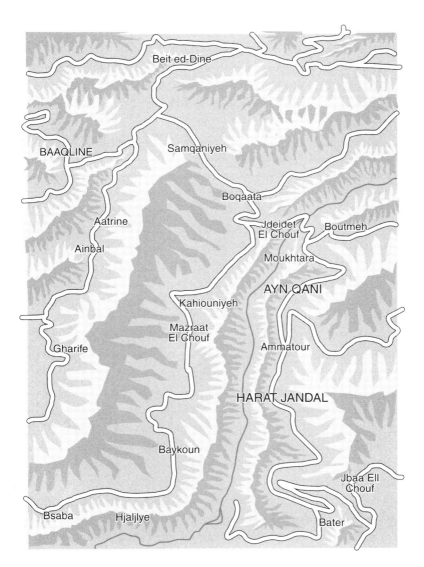

Map of Ayn Qani Region

During the restless years between 1903 and 1907, when the first car, telegraph, telephone, and tramway were introduced into the region, Said Bey was promoted to be head of the criminal court in Kumalinja, also in the Edirne Province.

In 1907, Said returned home to marry Hala al-Shaar from the neighboring hamlet of Harat Jandal. She was the only child of his father's ally Mahmud al-Shaar, the standard bearer of the Ottoman army.

The people of Ayn Qani accompanied the groom bearing gifts and sweetmeats. On arrival, the delegation faced the people of Harat Jandal and exchanged greetings. Said Bey, following Druze protocol, stood in the middle of the group and waited for his future father-in-law to bring him his fifteen-year-old bride. When the wedding rituals were done, Said Bey put Hala into a carriage and traveled with her the few miles that separated the two villages from each other and Hala from her family. A slip of a girl when she married the twenty-nine-year-old Said Bey, Hala attended the Nuns of Laazariya School in Beirut. Her Arabic, French, and Turkish were fluent.

The newly wed couple returned to Istanbul, and early in 1908 Nazira was born – since there were no birth certificates at the time there is no record of the date. The year 1908 was one of political upheaval throughout the region. Constitutional movements appeared in various parts of the Middle East, each striving to limit the power of autocratic regimes and to establish national rule. In October, the Young Turks staged a coup against Sultan 'Abd al-Hamid II who was deposed the following April. Turkism was the new creed. The focus of the Ottoman government turned east to Central Asia, and the Arab provinces took back stage to the Turkic regions. The "new policy of centralization and Turkification underlying the reform movement of the Young Turks alienated Muslim subjects of the Ottoman Empire and generated, as a reaction, a vigorous Arab nationalist sentiment" (Khalaf 1979, p. 138). Ethnic identity replaced Islam as a principle of political cohesion.

Said Bey's next post was in Aleppo, with its imposing citadel and world-famous market. It was his first posting in the Arab provinces of the Ottoman Empire. Shocked by the chaos, he set about cleaning up the corruption in the justice administration. He opened a night school for police and acquired a reputation for absolute honesty that was enthusiastically reported in the local papers (*Lubnan*, pp. 11–21). After a few months, he was transferred to Adana where Hala gave birth to a second daughter, whom they named Munira. It was there that Said Bey met the despotic Ottoman governor Jamal Pasha (1872–1922), aka the Slaughterer, for the first but not the last time.

In 1910, after a short stint in the Jerusalem court of appeals, he was posted to Beirut, and in February Hala gave birth to their first son, Munir – the date is known from a Turkish poem celebrating his birth (Bu Matar 2008, p. 16). The family stayed in the Lebanese capital until 1914, when Said Bey became embroiled in a scandal. Investigating the murder of a policeman whose killer could not be found, Said Bey pronounced innocent a Christian called Elias Rafful whom the Beirut police chief had imprisoned and wanted to execute. In multi-confessional Lebanon, tensions between the various communities often highlighted religious affiliations. That verdict earned Said Bey extravagant praise from the Lebanese and Egyptian press, but also Ottoman censure.

Said Bey and Hala packed their belongings into several horse-drawn carriages and left Beirut. Heading south out of town and along the coast beyond Damour to Mechref, they turned east and climbed up the spectacular serpentine road into the heart of the Chouf Mountains.

It was an arduous journey up the steep, unpaved road to Ayn Qani. They took with them their three children and the four Turkish slaves they had bought in Istanbul. With no idea of when or even whether they would return to the city, they spent the war years tucked away in their mountain mansion with its commanding view of the entire valley and neighboring Mukhtara, the palace of the powerful Jumblat clan (Bu Matar 2008, p. 24; *Lubnan*, pp. 32–52).

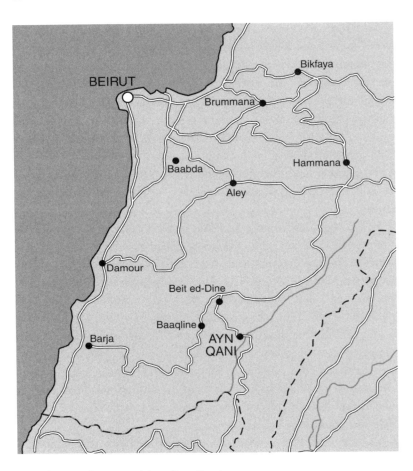

Map showing Beirut and Ayn Qani Region

Although World War I did not involve the Arab Middle East directly, its repercussions rippled throughout the region that "could not remain neutral." The Ottomans had allied themselves with the Germans in an attempt to counteract the growing influence of the British and French in the region (Schulze 2000, p. 41). They failed, but not without first inflicting great suffering.

The chief architect of this suffering was Jamal Pasha. In late 1914 he was sent to Lebanon to quash the opposition that was forming, and to occupy the mountain. He masterminded measures against Lebanese who had not cooperated in the Ottoman war effort,

> prohibiting shipments of wheat from the interior plains to the mountain areas. People suffered and many died from famine ... The villages had sufficient olive oil and fruit crops, but not enough grain crops and livestock. Also, the flow of foreign exchange from emigrants abroad was blocked and the famous silk industry of the village communities came to a standstill.
>
> (Tannous 2004, pp. 41, 74)

In 1915, the year of the Armenian genocide for which he was largely responsible, Jamal Pasha rounded up Syrian and Lebanese men to serve in the Ottoman army. The Safarbarlik, as this mobilization was called, left the women to deal with cholera and typhus epidemics, swarms of locusts, and a crippling famine that drove people to eat dogs and even to cannibalism. Cadavers of those who had died of starvation, said to be as many as 100,000, were thrown into mass graves. Historian Samir Khalaf describes Jamal Pasha's rule as the

> worst reign of terror the country had ever known. Until the end of the war, Lebanon was placed under Ottoman rule. Jamal Pasha imposed military conscription, requisitioned beasts of burden, and summoned people to relinquish much of their provisions to support his troops. Even trees, often entire groves, were cut down and used as fuel for army trains ... An infamous military court was established ... Evasion of military service, guilt by association or hearsay, membership in any of the burgeoning secret societies and clubs, and even a passing critical remark in a letter from a relative abroad were all punishable charges.
>
> (Khalaf 1979, p. 139)

In May 1916, Jamal Pasha executed twenty-one Syrian and Lebanese patriots. Fourteen men hanged in Beirut are the martyrs after whom the Place des Martyres in the middle of the Downtown is named (Tarabulsi 2008, pp. 123–124). The man who twenty-two years later was to become Nazira's husband, Shafiq al-Halabi, was on Jamal Pasha's death list; and he escaped just in time into the mountains.

Throughout these ordeals, Said Bey and his family were far from the capital. They shared their house with his brother Muhammad, his wife Amira, and their daughter Najla. It was here in 1917 that Hala gave birth to Kamil, their youngest child. For the four years of World War I the Zeineddines lived off the land, and Said Bey started a daily routine that he maintained until his death forty years later. Like the Jumblats and other Druze feudal lords, Said Bey invited to breakfast anyone who wanted to join him and his family. The house was open to peasants, *mashayikh,* and local leaders alike.

In the summer, the children slept on the upper terrace under tents made of laurel leaves. Years later, Samia Saab, Najla's daughter, described Said Bey's tent as made of "a very special material with

Ayn Qani Terrace

stripes. Jiddu slept on a high bed. Every morning at 6 sharp he would shout to Zaynab to bring his coffee, and we knew that it was time to get up." Said Bey called Zaynab, one of the Turkish servants, "rabibatna" or "the girl we raised." She in turn brought up all of his children and later his grandson Said. The children would collect around the long table that stretched the width of the terrace. For breakfast Farida, a Jewish maid, made sugar pancakes. After shaving him, Zaynab would hold a white parasol over him if the weather was sunny or a black umbrella if it rained. Farida held Amira's parasol. The children had to stay seated at the table until ten o'clock. *Mashayikh* came for advice and villagers for help, and for each he composed a lyric.

During the war years, Said Bey devoted himself to his family and the land. He planted orchards of apples and pears in the land, and the love of knowledge in the hearts of the children. He opened his home to the boys and girls of Ayn Qani, and he came to be known as *qadi bakhshish* or the judge who gave lessons, and sometimes also legal counsel, for free. At the time the Chouf had only eighteen schools for the 220 villages that were scattered in hard-to-reach places. The mode of transport was donkey, mule, or horse. For the children who attended the Zeineddine "school" from across the valleys, the walk was often long (Bu Matar 2008, p. 26). But his pride and joy was Nazira, for whom he clearly hoped great things. In the isolation of the mountains, Nazira and her sister Munira received instruction in Arabic and English from a Miss Qurban, and they spoke Turkish with the servants.

This mountain idyll, however, was not out of the reach of the Ottoman administration. The problem was Said's older brother Muhammad. In 1894, this outspoken judge had published poetry in Arabic and Turkish criticizing Ottoman policies in Lebanon, and especially the behavior of Jamal Pasha. In 1915, a year after Jamal Pasha became military governor of Lebanon, Muhammad was sent into exile in Turkey. When the family heard that Jamal Pasha was about to pass through Ayn Qani on his way to Jizzin, Said Bey and Muhammad's wife Amira came up with an intriguing scheme. Their daughters Nazira and Najla, aged seven and six, were to plead for the safe return of their uncle and father. Said Bey wrote a poem in Ottoman Turkish that he and Amira taught their daughters to recite. The reception for Jamal Pasha was extravagant, with drums, horns, and gunshots echoing across the valley. The governor listened to the cousins; his heart was said to have softened and he pardoned Muhammad (Bu Matar 2008, pp. 15–16, 27; Nuwayhid 1986, p. 171).

In December 1918, following the defeat of the Ottoman Empire, Jamal Pasha and his associates went into hiding in Switzerland, and Said Bey, whom the French had appointed prosecutor general, launched an investigation against them. He accused them of committing crimes against Syria and Lebanon in 1915, 1916, and 1917. They had extorted money, expelled civilians from their homes, jailed people without habeas corpus, and tortured and killed some under interrogation. Said Bey summoned the Ottoman henchmen for trial in March 1919. They did not respond to this summons nor to the one issued by a military court in Istanbul. Instead, Jamal Pasha escaped to Russian Caucasia where in 1922 an Armenian killed him. The French awarded Said Bey the Legion of Honor medal for his efforts to prosecute a war criminal (*Lubnan,* pp. 74–84).

All the while, the British and the French were dividing the region into individual nation-states under their control. Basing their claims on the 1916 Sykes–Picot Agreement ratified three years later in Versailles, the British took over Iraq, Jordan, and Palestine, and the French established their Mandate in Syria and Lebanon. The Mandate system opened up a new divide between the Druzes and the Muslims, especially the Sunni Muslims of Lebanon. Until that time, Druzes educated in Ottoman legal establishments were considered on a par with orthodox Muslims by virtue of their mastery of Islamic law. The arrival of the French exacerbated tensions between the communities, especially the Muslim communities, and eventually led to the drawing of hard lines between orthodox Sunnis and Shiites on the one hand and heterodox Druze Muslim sects on the other.

In 1920, Beirut became the headquarters of the French administration of the Levant States (Khalaf 1979, p. 140). While many Christians and some Druzes welcomed the French, the Sunnis and

Shiites did not. They were particularly opposed to the 1920 French declaration of the State of Greater Lebanon that put them under the jurisdiction of the Maronites, the French protégés who controlled Mount Lebanon.

Not only were the Europeans acquiring control of the countries to the east of the Mediterranean, they were also conspiring to implant a new nation-state in the region. In 1917, the Balfour Declaration confirmed European commitment to the establishment of a Jewish state, probably on the land of Palestine. In 1925, writes Lebanese educator Wadad al-Maqdisi Qurtas (1909–1979), when Lord Balfour was expected to visit Lebanon on his way to Palestine, there was such an outcry that he had to travel under cover of darkness (Qurtas 1982, pp. 54–55).

Qurtas' memoirs describe a post-war Beirut full of Palestinians, Syrians, Egyptians, Sudanese, and Iraqis who had moved there for their children's education since there were better schools and colleges in Beirut than in their own countries. But she also remembers "a terrifying stream" of British and French soldiers marching through the streets of Beirut armed to the teeth (pp. 35, 45). Resistance to the Europeans intensified. The Americans were considered less hostile, and so in 1922 the League of Nations authorized the King–Crane Commission to conduct an investigation. It concluded that the French should not intervene in the affairs of Arab communities because of racist policies in their North African colonies, their political expediency in only supporting local Catholics, their hypocrisy, their immoral literature, and an educational system that corrupted women (see the Confidential Appendix of King–Crane Commission Report, originally printed in *Editor & Publisher*, Vol. 55, No. 27, 2nd Section, 2 December 1922).

Small wonder that the establishment of the French Mandate sparked resistance movements in Muslim-majority areas, especially in Syria. Between 1925 and 1927, the Druze Sultan Pasha al-Atrash (1891–1982) and his brother Emir Hasan al-Atrash led the Syrian Druze in a rebellion that the French crushed. Out of a total population of 300,000, 6,000 were killed.

Emir Hasan was the father of Nina al-Atrash (b. 1952), cousin by marriage of the younger Said Zeineddine, who spent time with Nazira during the early 1970s. Emir Hasan al-Atrash's marriage to Nina's mother Linda Jumblat sealed a union between the Syrian al-Atrash and the Lebanese Jumblat clans. Of the nine women her father had married consecutively – the Druzes do not practice polygyny – one was the singer Asmahan (1917–1944) with whom Nazira struck up a lifelong friendship.

Even if the Druze revolt failed militarily, historian Abbas El Halabi suggests that it should be acknowledged as having succeeded politically: "It was at this moment that Lebanon's first

Nazira and Asmahan (courtesy of Said Zeineddine)

constitution was elaborated. In spring 1926 the first Lebanese republic with a parliamentary system was declared" (al-Halabi 2005, pp. 79, 227). Although the Lebanese would not win their independence from the French for another seventeen years, they had sowed the seeds.

3

ISLAMIC LESSONS

W hen Said Bey was appointed first president of the court of appeals, the Zeineddine family moved into a red tiled two-storey stone house in Karakol Druze.

Like Ayn Qani, this house was open to guests. Eager to learn about other religions and esoteric philosophies, Said Bey turned their house into "a gathering place for intellectuals and scholars from all religions in Beirut and elsewhere." Guests included Sunnis, Shiites, Christians, and, of course, Druzes (Bu Matar 2008, p. 16).

Nazira and Munira were sent to Catholic schools with girls from the Lebanese Christian elite. Between 1918 and 1920, they attended

Nazira (fourth from left) outside Karakol Druze house (courtesy of Said Zeineddine)

the local primary school of St. Joseph de l'Apparition and then for six years the Sisters of Nazareth Convent School. They were the first Druze girls to gain admission to this school. The nuns exposed them to French culture and to philosophers like Rousseau, Montesquieu, and the English John Stuart Mill, and to new ideas about the roles and rights of women that were being debated in Europe. French was the language of instruction, and the nuns frowned on any use of Lebanese Arabic, the idiom of the street.

Those who rejected a colonial education, like Wadad Qurtas' parents, might send their daughters to the nationalist Ahliya School. In 1921 the French authorities ordered Ahliya to be closed. A teacher and student demonstration and protest to the high commissioner succeeded in staying the closure but did not avert the order to double instruction in French language and culture at the expense of the Arabic language and Lebanese history. As a nationalist symbol, Ahliya attracted some high-level visitors, including women involved in the burgeoning feminist movement, women such as Julia Dimashqiya,

Nazira and Munira in Beirut 1920 (courtesy of Said Zeineddine)

Nazik al-Abid Bayhum (future leader of the Arab Women Workers' Union), and Mayy Ziyada. Qurtas writes that Ahliya students "engaged in violent debates with boys and girls in foreign schools who were not accustomed to self-respect or to appreciation of their language and history" (Qurtas 1982, pp. 46–49). The Zeineddine girls seem to have been unaware of this nationalist ferment at the other end of town.

Nazira lived between two worlds, negotiating the spaces between the liberal atmosphere of home and school and the conservative street. Although she was Druze and attended Catholic schools, she was unambiguous about her religious identity: she insisted that she was "a *Muslim* girl whom faith has enlightened. I grew up in an elite, intellectual environment, attending a variety of schools and colleges," all of which were French and Catholic (*The Girl and the Shaykhs*, p. 19). At the time, the coming split between Sunnis and Shiites on the one hand and Druzes on the other was not yet felt.

As a teenager, Nazira was already interested in women's issues and she worked for the Lebanese Women's Union. When the Union later consolidated twenty-nine women's organizations into the Syrian-Lebanese Women's Union, she participated in codifying its constitution.

While Munira did not study beyond the convent school, Nazira was eager to pursue her education. Her application to the Jesuit medical school of St. Joseph was – not unexpectedly – turned down since the institution was for men only and she knew it. Yet she was disappointed because she had set her heart on becoming a doctor in a society where too many women died unnecessarily because they refused to be treated by male doctors (Bu Matar 2008, p. 29). The obvious answer was to train women doctors, but the Lebanese were not yet ready for such a drastic step. It was only in the early 1930s that the first Lebanese women doctors graduated from the American University medical school.

A short stay at the American University that accepted few women at the time (Qurtas 1982, p. 71) convinced Nazira that this was no place for her. She was explicit about her reaction to a place full of the

Lebanese middle classes and recent Arab immigrants. The atmosphere was too proletarian for this refined young woman who spoke four languages and whose father mixed with the French and Beirut elite. It is ironic that someone with such social pretensions should become known for her social activism. Instead Nazira chose another French institution, the Lycée Français Laique, a co-ed high school. In 1928 she graduated among the top in her class, outdoing even her French male classmates. She was the first Lebanese woman to earn a French Baccalaureate in literature and Arabic.

At home Nazira studied Islamic scriptures with her father. Said Bey taught her the intricacies of the texts, how they worked, what they allowed, and what they forbad. He read her stories about the life of the Prophet Muhammad and of the women and men who joined the nascent movement in the seventh century. These stories, that included the words and actions of the Prophet reported by his Companions, were called Traditions. They functioned like moral guide-posts, influencing individual choices in all spheres of life, and Muhammad's Companions were the authoritative sources whose witness to his actions and speeches formed the heart of a burgeoning legal system. With the Qur'an, they provided the foundations for the various schools of jurisprudence that were to emerge over the following two to three centuries. So crucial were these exemplary stories and sayings that they shaped the believer's behavior and life. Whoever could cite a Tradition felt empowered to act like the Prophet and to compel others to do so.

"The problem with these Traditions," Said Bey explained during one of their sessions together, "is that even during his lifetime some of Muhammad's Companions claimed to have heard or seen the Prophet say or do something he clearly had not said or done. And when this happened, the Prophet himself would intervene: 'People lie about me. Whenever they say anything contradicting the Qur'an, I didn't say it. Any Tradition that is not consonant with the Qur'an is false. Whoever deliberately lies about me will find a place in hell.' … Everything goes back to the Qur'an and God's commands and prohibitions and whatever does not accord with God's Book is false"

(*Unveiling and Veiling*, pp. 66, 239). Soon after Muhammad's death, false Traditions proliferated. It was enough to cite some chain of authorities back to a supposed witness for an individual to authorize some attitude and then transform it into a mandate.

"The Traditions were not written down during the life of the Prophet lest they be confused with the written words of the Qur'an," Said Bey continued. "For over one hundred and fifty years the Traditions were transmitted orally, and with the lapse of so much time human memory can betray. Stories passed on from one generation to another are susceptible to change" (*Unveiling and Veiling*, pp. 234, 235). By the ninth century, there were hundreds of thousands of Traditions.

Said Bey devoted several lessons to the two ninth-century scholars, Abu 'Abdallah al-Bukhari and Muslim ibn al-Hajjaj, who devised a way to distinguish the weak and false Traditions in circulation at the time from the sound, or *sahih*, ones. "They sifted through 360,000 Traditions to come up with no more than 10,000 sound ones, thereby invalidating 350,000" (*Unveiling and Veiling*, p. 234). These two compilations of sound Traditions, known as *Sahih Bukhari* and *Sahih Muslim* or *The Two Sound Ones,* became the foundation for the Islamic legal system, but even they were not infallible.

"What Bukhari and Muslim did almost a thousand years ago was a beginning. They chose the few Traditions that seemed demonstrably true. I say 'seemed' because even if the chain of authorities was perfect there were still some that weren't quite right. The fact that a Tradition may be found in one of these two texts," Said Bey insisted, "does not mean that it's above scrutiny. Even authenticated Traditions have been shown to be false. And, of course, the fabrication of Traditions did not stop with Bukhari and Muslim, so that by the twelfth century the great theologian and mystic Imam al-Ghazali could claim that 70,000 were false" (*Unveiling and Veiling*, p. 66).

Nazira learned how to dissect chains of authority for particular Traditions and how to verify an action or a saying attributed to Muhammad. Having learned that much of the law, of an Islamic sense of justice and truth was based on the Traditions these two men had authenticated, she had to question what she had just committed to memory.

Said Bey elaborated: "Take, for example, the Tradition people like to cite concerning the prohibition on women's education, especially their right to write. A certain al-Shihab ibn Hajar was said to have cited: 'Do not bring women down into the chambers and do not teach them to write' – most judges believe that this Tradition is forged because it contradicts God's Book" (*Unveiling and Veiling*, p. 234).

"What if the Tradition does not contradict something in the Qur'an because there is nothing in the Qur'an on the subject?" Nazira asked. "How can we check if it is sound?"

"You should look for bias. If there are Traditions that consistently favor one group of people, you need to think about the identity of this group. If the interpreters are from one region and that region is favored, then you know that this is not necessarily the truth but perhaps regional chauvinism. If the interpreters are men, they may prefer verses that privilege men's rights and status at women's expense. Wasn't it possible for Bukhari and Muslim as male interpreters to opt, even if subconsciously, for those Traditions that had Muhammad say or do something that empowered men?" (*The Girl and the Shaykhs*, p. 42).

"Isn't that unbelief? Religious authorities wouldn't do something like that, would they? Haven't centuries of scholarship established their choices as correct?"

"Nazira, there are a couple of things you must learn. First, if jurisprudence does not accord with the welfare of the *umma* and also with reason then the interpretations must be wrong. Why? Because interpretations are subjective and can be right or wrong according to the circumstances surrounding the life and personality of the interpreters and also depending on the time and place in which they are produced. Everything goes back to the Qur'an and the Sunna (*Unveiling and Veiling*, p. 76). Second, never accept anything without thinking about it first. Even what we consider the most sacred is, indeed must remain, open to the believing, inquiring mind. God gave

us all, regardless of race, gender and power, the same ability to reason and to criticize. If we follow others blindly, repeating verbatim
what we hear, we are abusing the most precious gift God bestowed
upon humanity."

"Can women interpret religious texts?"

"Of course, why do you ask?"

"I have heard some shaykhs cite a Tradition from Bukhari's
Sound volume 1, book 6, #301 that women are deficient in reason
and religion."

"Rubbish!" he snapped impatiently.

Nazira was quiet.

"This is exactly what I have been trying to tell you. Bukhari may
have included it in his *Sound* but it is so contradictory with the Qur'an
that it cannot be correct. If Muhammad told his followers that they
should take half their religion from his wife Aisha that obviously
means that she, and consequently other women, could not be
deficient in religion and reason" (*Unveiling and Veiling*, pp.101–103).
Nazira was intrigued. Sinking back into the brocade chair she
looked at this man, her father, the judge. He was in a world of his own
where centuries of scholars were in constant conversation with
each other.

Nazira loved the book-lined study with its orange-red Moroccan
leather-bound volumes waiting for the curious to pull them off the
shelves. But Said Bey let few touch them. The study was a ritual
space for the initiated. Nazira sat across from him, separated by the
majestic mother-of-pearl inlaid desk. Sometimes it was piled high
with books and papers; at other times it was stark and clean, except
for the brass ashtray brimming over with cigarette and cigar butts.
The room smelt good.

"Do you know how many Traditions there are about Muhammad's
exhortations to his Companions to respect and elevate women? They
are countless. When you next hear someone pronounce this absur-
dity you should challenge him and say, 'O, you who claim to follow
the model of the prophets, where did you excavate the idea about
women's deficiency in religion and reason that has led you astray?

Beware lest you betray this precious treasure.'" Nazira smiled at her father's quaint language but years later she would remember these words and repeat them (*Unveiling and Veiling*, p. 95).

"Father, where do these scholars get their arguments about male superiority in religion and reason?"

"They are based on Qur'anic verses that grant women half a man's right to inheritance and consider women's witness worth only half that of a man. Polygyny and repudiation, or men's unilateral right to a divorce without trial, have played their part," Said Bey explained, and went on to argue against these supposed rights. "It is quite clear that God hates repudiation because it is a denial of grace and a destruction of homes. Remember what our great Imam al-Ghazali said over eight hundred years ago: 'Repudiation is only permitted if there is no unnecessary harm, but the mere fact of its possibility entails harm.' As for the matter of Muslim women's witness being half that of a Muslim man, there's an obvious problem. If that is indeed the case, what are we to make of the law disallowing the witness of non-Muslims? Does that mean that all non-Muslims are mentally inferior? Surely not! Anyhow, Hanafi law has long considered Muslim women's witness in most criminal cases to be equal to that of men. Moreover, the new Turkish state has just banned polygyny, thereby confirming our Druze belief that men should be monogamous. Ataturk's government has also granted women equal rights to testify and to inherit land" (*Unveiling and Veiling*, pp. 96, 220).

"Shouldn't this equality be extended to inheritance of other goods?"

"Of course! As you well know, in his Book God enjoined upon men to pay their brides a dower that should be of a substantial amount, enough to guarantee a woman's independent subsistence in case of divorce. Additionally, men are required to provide adequate support for the needs of women and children. The costs of the dower and lifelong support amount to much more than half an inheritance because they are on-going through the life of a woman whereas the inheritance is a one-time sum" (*Unveiling and Veiling*, pp. 97, 100).

She had no doubt that in God's eyes men and women were equal in every way and above all in intellect, because the Qur'an is full of verses about God giving reason equally to women and men. Later, she would cite many Qur'anic verses, often together for emphasis, about gender equality in intellect so that her readers could understand and act in accordance with scripture and revelation. It is in her eloquent polemic in defense of gender equality in intellect that she may be considered to have charted a new path in Islamic feminism.

To use one's mind does not mean that one will necessarily join some kind of consensus; Muhammad is reported to have said "disagreement among the various schools of thought in my nation is a mercy for them" (*Unveiling and Veiling*, p. 30). In all her writings, Nazira would insist on the need for independent reasoning when dealing with matters of faith. Her plea to women to develop individual powers of reasoning and not to obey blindly the dictates of the shaykhs came first from her father.

"The men in the family relied on the women," Samia Saab explained the norms in the Zeineddine household from the time she was a child. "They wanted the women to be outspoken because they could say what the men could not. It was almost as though they were daring the women to be outrageous."

Nazira was also indebted to modernist reformers like Iranian Jamal al-Din al-Afghani (1839–1897), and the Egyptians Muhammad 'Abduh (1849–1905), and Qasim Amin who had said that Islam demands the use of reason; faith without reason was not true faith (*Unveiling and Veiling*, pp. 71, 105).

Above all, she shared the Druze belief in the supremacy of *'aql,* intellect or reason, and respect for women. But for her this was not a Druze belief but a Shiite pillar of faith; she called it the fourth pillar and repeatedly equated the *'aql* with *ruh* or spirit that is essential to the humanness of all human beings (*The Girl and the Shaykhs,* pp. 370–374). The historian El Halabi explains that at the top of the Druze hierarchy is the Universal Intellect and then the Universal Soul. The spiritual leader of the Druze community is called *Shaykh 'aql,* or the Grand Intellect. Women and men become *'aqil* after proving that they have "tamed their being and mastered their material passions for a long period ... Some choose to remain chaste in their marriage in order to live a kind of mortification of the flesh ... [women play an important role in Druze society] wives share with their husbands in making important decisions concerning the family ... Boys and girls benefit from the same education" (El Halabi 2005, pp. 45, 85–87, 90–92, 95, see also Hirschberg 1969, pp. 345–346).

Yes, Nazira had received the best secular education money could buy in the Lebanon of the 1920s, and she had gone through a kind of religious boot camp with her father. She was, in fact, much more conversant with the Islamic sciences than either of her two brothers, whose Arabic teacher, Jamil Fakhuri, later became her chief editor.

4

RELIGIOUS INTERLOCUTORS

Whenever possible, Nazira joined one of the many gatherings in the Zeineddine homes either in Karakol Druze or in Ayn Qani. She relished the moments of exchange and debate, unafraid to confront the Sunni shaykhs when she disagreed with what they said. One of these visitors was Shaykh Mustafa al-Ghalayini (1886–1944), president of the Lebanese court of justice for the Muslim minority and a professor at the Islamic College of Beirut. He was a dapper forty-year-old when Nazira first met him. He was clean-shaven except for a narrow mustache, and wore tailored suits, well-knotted ties, and a red fez. He was impeccably polite to Hala and her two daughters, but when Nazira overstayed her welcome in the parlor where the men were meeting, he would indicate his displeasure.

Offended, Nazira decided to learn more about this religious scholar whom her father admired for his progressive views on women but who was intolerant of his colleague's wife and daughters. He was to become Nazira's greatest critic and her favorite target. After reading his *Islam Spirit of Civilization; or the Islamic Religion and Lord Cromer* (1908), she was blunt about its confusion and contradictions between progressive ideas and extreme misogyny. He was a constant subject of discussion with her father who defended the scholar if not the man.

"Nazira, you have to give him credit for pointing out that the face veil is not religious but a holdover from pre-Islamic times. He has written that 'the Prophet freed women from their bonds of absolute slavery so that they might acquire a high position in the family and were given rights that made them equal to men in everything except in authority and governance'."

"I have no doubt that he's proud of women's greater equality in Islam than in other monotheistic religions," Nazira replied. "But then he blithely contradicts himself. Listen to this: 'It is impossible to combine notions of their freedom and independence with respect and honor for women. The reason is that women's independence infringes upon men's centrality and freedom; consequently men will hate this situation and they will be compelled to despise and disrespect women because men are physically stronger and more rational ... By their nature men refuse to submit to women's control; neither men nor women will be content with that situation and it will lead to mutual repugnance ... As long as women spend three quarters, if not nine tenths of their time on clothes and primping and the remaining tenth chatting about them they cannot demand a single right that men claim'" (*Unveiling and Veiling*, p. 270).

"No, Shaykh al-Ghalayini is wrong. He should read John Stuart Mill for whom women's preoccupation with their bodies is a compensation for lack of control over their own lives." She found Mill's *The Subjection of Women* on the top shelf of her bookcase: "those to whom others will not leave the undisturbed management of their own affairs, will compensate themselves, if they can, by meddling for their own purposes with the affairs of others. Hence women's passion for personal beauty and dress and display" (Mill 1869, p. 51).

"Do you not know that women's freedom and independence are rights?" she once asked Shaykh al-Ghalayini during a visit to their Karakol Druze house. "When you wrote about women's inferiority you claimed that men's strength was the reason for their greater reason and acumen. What's the connection between reason and physical strength? Over fifty years ago, John Stuart Mill refuted the primitive 'might is right' law, saying that 'the banishment of that primitive law commenced the regeneration of human nature' [Mill, pp. 3–4]. Men claim superiority because of their strength, but they can only do so by making sure that women stay weak.

"I have to say I'm puzzled. Sometimes you write about men's tyranny and their refusal to acknowledge women's achievements. You've deplored the mistreatment of women in the pre-Islamic period, mentioning in particular female infanticide and rampant polygyny. You've gone so far as to say that before Islam women were considered to be no more than animals. On p. 272, you wrote that the Sharia 'calls for a woman's obedience to her husband except when that obedience interferes with her search for knowledge at which point she need not obey him but should go in search of knowledge. She should study whatever makes her happy in the two lives (here and the hereafter).' You have written that religion has commanded that a woman should be educated and cultivated like a man.

"So how can you then advocate the suppression of women's rights after condemning men's ignorance and tyranny over women and their neglect of the rights granted women in the Sharia? Did you not say that the sin is in the men and not in the religion? Following Muhammad who said 'the path to paradise is knowledge,' you cite dozens of Traditions about the importance of knowledge for all, women included. Yet elsewhere you advocate women's submission with the pretext that it enhances the welfare of the Umma. Surely, it's the opposite. The Prophet often said the oppression of the weak by the strong was wrong; it angered God" (*Unveiling and Veiling*, pp. 83, 84, 89, 230–231, 273, 277).

Taken aback by the girl's boldness and meticulous reading of his book, Shaykh al-Ghalayini muttered a few words that she interrupted impatiently.

"God Almighty commanded us to swear allegiance to the Prophet so that he might teach us the roots of popular or democratic rule in which both men and women should participate. Remember that the Prophet (peace be upon him) had once said: 'One good woman is better than a thousand bad men'" (*Unveiling and Veiling*, p. 281). When addressing a religious authority, Nazira would affix the "peace be upon him" to any mention of the Prophet in order to affirm her piety.

"Yes, you are right." In spite of himself, the Shaykh found himself drawn into conversation with Nazira. "But the problem is with *fitna*, or the seductiveness of women; it is the cause of the worst evil in the world."

"Women, my dear Sir, are more seductive when veiled and enticingly unavailable. As for evil in the world, you know as well as I that women have not been involved in the evil and wars that men like Attila, Tamerlane, Genghis Khan, and Nero have perpetrated. Naturally inclined to nursing, their participation has been limited to binding wounds, reducing pain and staunching blood. How can you accuse women of greater evil when you know they make up only 1% of prison populations?" (*Unveiling and Veiling*, pp.196, 282, 283).

The Shaykh looked over at his colleague, expecting him to stop his daughter. How dare this teenager interrogate and lecture him? But Said Bey was looking at his daughter in admiration.

"Have you forgotten Muhammad's first wife Khadija, Mother of the Faithful and the first to believe our Prophet? She was the one who enabled the light of the prophetic dawn to shine. From the beginning it was she who was his strongest supporter. Who saved Moses from death? Wasn't it a woman? Wasn't it Pharaoh's daughter? Who was the first to believe in Moses' message? Wasn't it a woman? Wasn't it Assia bint Muzahim? Remember how Pharaoh bound her arms and legs to posts and commanded a large rock to be thrown down on her while she was shouting 'Dear God, build me a house in your paradise.' How can you say that women are the source of evil when they count among their numbers the Virgin Mary, Fatima al-Zahra, Khadija Mother of the Faithful, and the red-haired Aisha? How can you say what you say about women when it is they who give birth to prophets?" (*Unveiling and Veiling*, pp. 283–284).

The room was thick with silence. Shaykh al-Ghalayini was frowning and breathing hard. Leafing through *Islam Spirit of Civilization*, Nazira read aloud to the stunned Shaykh his own words: "The veil in its current fashion is not indicated in the Qur'an or in the Sound Traditions. Muslims have borrowed it from peoples who were their neighbors. Islamic law disapproves of today's veil; it calls upon men to avert their gaze from women. Whoever considers today's veil will see that it is more seductive than the uncovered face" (*Unveiling and Veiling*, pp. 197, 201).

"Were these not your words?" Bright red in the face, the Shaykh did not answer.

"My dear guide," her tongue dripped sarcasm, "you are afraid of women's knowledge; you are afraid to remove the covering from her heart just as you are afraid to remove the veil from her eyes. It seems that you want her heart and eyes to remain blind so that she will be a dumb instrument in the hands of someone like you" (*Unveiling and Veiling*, p. 225).

"So, Papa, what did you think about his reaction?" she asked after the Shaykh had taken a hurried leave. "He couldn't answer, could he? He is a hypocrite talking out of both sides of his mouth at once. On the one hand, he is writing to Lord Cromer in Egypt and boasting about his feminist religion and telling the British how many more rights Muslim women have than their Christian sisters. On the other hand, he is addressing women who might take him at his word to the British consul-general that their religion empowers them and considers them equal to men. While telling the British colonizer to stop interfering in the religious life of the people with the pretext of saving women from rampant misogyny, al-Ghalayini is telling us to remain submissive to these same misogynist men!

"I am so glad I could finally tell him what I think. Anyway I am not saying anything new. The Egyptian and local magazines and papers are full of articles making the same arguments. It is so exciting! People called the end of the last century the age of electricity; and I have no doubt that my grandchildren will call this period the age of women" (*Unveiling and Veiling*, p. 283).

"Well, if you have anything to do with it, they certainly will! That was quite some speech," Said Bey beamed.

"Anyone in their right mind can see that the injustice done to women is in clear contravention of God's Book, the Sunna, the Prophet Muhammad, and reason itself. The irrational have strayed from what is clearly good because they are ignorant of the welfare of the Umma. The more I read these men and listen to the likes of this Shaykh the angrier I get" (*Unveiling and Veiling*, pp. 39–40).

"You shouldn't be so harsh on al-Ghalayini. Nazira, you have not taken into account that part of the problem might be that he wrote his book nineteen years ago. It came out in 1908. That, my child, is the year you were born." He smiled wistfully, "He's better than most."

"No, he's not. All he cares about is his image and trumpeting the glories of his religion without understanding it. He wants to boast to the West about how great Muhammad was and what a feminist. This is not because he cares a fig for actual women and their status and treatment today. It's all about him, the nationalist feminist who hates women! That's why he keeps contradicting himself. His point is that he is a member of the world's best religion, better than any other religion of the Book. One of the reasons his religion is the best is because its founder honored women. It is modern and nationalist to be feminist. That's what you said yourself last time he was here.

"I will refute these shaykhs so that the world will know that it is neither Islam nor men in general that deprive women of their rights. The problem is with the shaykhs who abuse their authority to make people believe whatever suits them. Men like you are our strongest allies. In fact, I am going to write a book and dedicate it to you because it will be a reflection of the rays from the light of your knowledge and the freedom of your will and thought" (*Unveiling and Veiling*, p. 37).

Without realizing it, Nazira had declared war on the shaykhs, with Mustafa al-Ghalayini in the front line. That confrontation did not end with the Shaykh's hurried departure. He was, after all, now prepared for her book.

Her first chance to reach a public came in 1927 when she addressed an audience at her school, the Lycée Français Laique. The title of her lecture was "Why Girls Should be Educated." Before giving the talk she checked with her father and he brought in Jamil Fakhuri, her brothers' Arabic tutor, to make sure the language was impeccable

(Bu Matar 2008, p. 30). Then she delivered her message: women cannot perform the duties expected of them if they are not educated. This lecture, delivered on consecutive days, first to men and then to women, was the first block in the building of her book.

In early 1928, the Sunni scholar, Taqi al-Din al-Sulh, later to become prime minister, invited her to deliver her second lecture at the Arab Literary Association over which he presided. She agreed to give a talk entitled "Why I prefer unveiling to veiling." Again, she checked with her father who in turn checked with his good friend Shaykh Yusuf al-Faqih, president of the Jaafari Shiite court. During one of his visits to their Karakol Druze house, Nazira asked her father to read the Shaykh her lecture. After listening carefully he declared himself satisfied, with the caveat that there were not enough citations from religious sources, and he gave her some books to read. It was not enough to be logical and reasoned in her insistence that there was no Islamic mandate for the veil. Intelligence, he explained, was not sufficient qualification to speak about such matters. Before uttering any opinion about any issue of Islamic concern, she would have to read all the canonical texts (Bu Matar 2008, p. 38). She followed his advice and amplified the lecture with extensive quotations.

Before accepting al-Sulh's invitation to address the Arab Literary Association, she stipulated that she would only do so if the women in the audience did not cover their faces and could sit next to the men. Taqi al-Din al-Sulh acceded to her wishes and made a point of inviting 'Anbara Salam. In 1921, she had given a provocative demonstration of the problem with the face veil. Addressing an audience with her face covered, 'Anbara launched into her lecture. Protests arose from the audience. They couldn't hear her; she should remove the veil. She complied with alacrity, and her lecture became the occasion for the "first public lecture by an unveiled woman before men in either Syria or Lebanon" (Thompson 2000, p.136; see also Nuwayhid 1986, pp. 353–357). Knowing who was in the audience, Nazira cited approvingly a lecture 'Anbara had delivered after living in England for two years about how well unveiled English women were treated.

Nazira's lecture was a great success, and Taqi al-Din al-Sulh was delighted. Later, when the book came out, he called on young women to uncover their faces and to take part in the awakening launched by the "Zeineddine girl" whose valuable book provided guidance, not evil (*The Girl and the Shaykhs*, p. 104).

After the success of these lectures, she gave several more in public venues like the Grand Theatre of Beirut. These public talks became chapters in the book. From June 1927 until March 1928, she wrote day after day, week after week, allowing her pen to follow what she called "her soul in pain" (*The Girl and the Shaykhs*, p. 12). She realized that many of the people she wanted to reach, particularly the shaykhs, would not listen to her in a hall full of women. They would judge her without understanding what she was saying. With a book it would be different, she hoped, because they would have to read before dismissing her arguments – or so she thought (*The Girl and the Shaykhs*, p. 183).

"I gave my reason full liberty and I received from the Qur'an and the Sunna guidance concerning freedom and women's rights whose light was so intense, it would shame the brightness of the sun when it rises" (*Unveiling and Veiling*, p. 76).

This transcendental guidance led her to pen hundreds of pages arguing for women's intellectual capacities and against the veil that rendered women invisible and deprived them of value and basic human rights. She could not understand how the shaykhs could believe that the veil was more impervious to change than all the other religious prescriptions that they had modified or eliminated over time (*Unveiling and Veiling*, p. 82). Why was it that the Syrian shaykhs insisted on the veil when in Egypt and Turkey the opponents of the veil had won? Why did they reject women judges and religious inter-preters when Muhammad had accepted them? In answer, she cited Ibrahim Hafiz's elegy for Qasim Amin, the Egyptian judge and author of *The Liberation of Women*. After praising Amin, Hafiz, aka the Poet of the Nile, lampoons the shaykhs who were so obstinate that even if Eve their foremother and the Virgin Mary were to appear before them with their faces uncovered as proof that women should not veil they would not believe. Even if Moses, Jesus, and Muhammad supported these iconic women and explained that God allowed women to reveal their faces and to mix with men and that doing so was not in contravention of divine commands, these shaykhs would reject them; they would refuse to believe the highest religious authorities (*Unveiling and Veiling*, pp. 136, 201–202). This religious mafia was so self-satisfied that nothing could shake their convictions. Nazira knew this to be the case and yet she was determined to try. She would be the first modern woman to step into the closed circuit of the shaykhs' world.

The feminist ferment in Egypt seemed to augur well for Muslim women in the region, but then some alarming news reached Lebanon. A new religious group was forming under the leadership of a young charismatic leader called Hasan al-Banna' (1906–1949). A twenty-one-year-old graduate of Dar al-Ulum and an elementary school teacher, he was gathering around him men who shared his concern about the British occupation of his country and the moral degradation of Muslim societies. In March of 1928, just as she was finishing her book, they launched their movement called the Muslim Brothers. They called for a jihad to cleanse the *umma* from within. Years of living under European colonial rule had deviated Egyptians and Muslims in general from the Straight Path. The Brothers were to be among the leaders of the anti-colonial movements that spread around the Arab world during the 1930s. They feared that Ataturk's secular revolution in Turkey would infect the Arab world. Something had to be done. They focused on women, wanting them to be the educated but conservative vanguard of a new, reformed Islam. Women who called for unveiling were labeled shameless, those wanting suffrage were said to have sold out to the French, and the first girls to matriculate in the Egyptian University in 1928 were censored (al-Jawhari 2007, pp. 278–279).

When she heard about the Brothers and their ideas concerning reform and women, Nazira was alarmed. Their obsession with women and their role in upholding the morality of the society did not augur well for women's awakening. Even though they claimed to be reformers, they seemed to be allied with the retrograde Syrian and Lebanese shaykhs who were screaming for the veil.

Eagerly, she read women's journals and everything that feminists such as Lebanese-Palestinian Mayy Ziyada and Egyptian Malak Hifni Nasif were writing. And for every article that a woman wrote in defense of women's rights in Islam and against the religious mandate to veil, shaykhs responded with disquisitions about women's duties that were reduced to a piece of cloth over the face.

"They are sending us back to the Middle Ages!" she exclaimed.

"They" were shaykhs like Said al-Baghdadi, Ibrahim al-Qayati al-Azhari, Mustafa Rahim al-Tarabulsi, Salim Hamdan, Said Abas, Mahmud al-Shamitili, Ahmad Muhyi al-Din al-Azhari, Salah al-Din al-Zaim, Said al-Jabi, 'Abd al-Qadir al-Kirmani, 'Abdallah 'Alayini, and, of course, Mustafa al-Ghalayini! After the publication of *Unveiling and Veiling* this rogues' gallery of opponents would produce pages, articles, and even books refuting her thesis (*The Girl and the Shaykhs*, p. 251).

One evening in late winter of 1927, Said Bey went to the house of the Mufti of Beirut, Muhammad 'Umar Naja (d.1932), where a number of intellectuals were gathered. Nazira had asked her father to consult with the Mufti to make sure that she was on the right track. Said Bey read some pages to the men. The Mufti liked what he heard and he sent his praise and congratulations.

Some time later the Mufti, Ibrahim al-Majdub, and the feudal lord Sami Bey Jumblat visited Said Bey. Conversation turned to the book she had almost finished. Apparently unable to enter the room when these particular men were present, she followed the proceedings from the room next door. Later, she would remind the Mufti Muhammad 'Umar Naja of that visit.

"I'll never forget how you and the honorable Shaykh Ibrahim al-Majdub honored our house and read my book when it was written and just before it was published. I overheard my father read to you many of its pages … You called out to me in congratulation. I can still hear your words of pleasure ringing in my ears and I am proud of them. When the reading was done you said to my father, repeating

the praise you had uttered several times during the reading: 'May
God preserve and bless her. I don't agree with her on the matter of
unveiling, because I believe the face should be covered even if not
with the current transparent and enticing veil. But she did argue
from God's Book and the Traditions of the Prophet and there is no
blame in what she concluded from her interpretation.'

"Then, Shaykh Ibrahim turned to my father: 'Can't you convince
her to turn the power of her argument, her evidence, and her broad
knowledge to a defense of the veil?'

"How can I ever forget that it was you, the Mufti, who interjected,
'Shaykh Ibrahim, you've already been told that a large part of the
book has been printed, so why do you ask such a thing? It is enough
that she has understood the principles of religion and knows how to
interpret scriptures. Moreover, she has condemned women who
primp or expose themselves and has warned against moral depravity
and frequenting places of ill repute. As for unveiling the face, she has
her opinion and we have ours. All should have their own opinions and
beliefs.'" (*The Girl and the Shaykhs*, pp. 91–95)

The Mufti then told everyone in the room to read the book and
recommend it to others. Others also expressed admiration for the
young woman. Satisfied with their approval, she sent the manuscript
to Quzma Press.

THE BOOK

Freedom and equality are the two major themes of *Unveiling and Veiling*, a book that summarized her Islamic lessons and demonstrated her profound grasp of women's religiously sanctioned rights. The very first sentence exhorts women to remove the cover from their sight and insight so that they might see the flood of freedom God has granted. Five Qur'anic verses follow, each telling individuals to make their own decisions with God as guide. Those who unquestioningly follow parents with a pre-Islamic conscience should not be surprised to find themselves in hell. That is the law of Islam: each is responsible for her own virtues and vices; no one has the right to interfere in the lives of others (*Unveiling and Veiling*, pp. 39, 55, 63, 35).

Nazira addresses men, with whispered asides to women. She may write "Gentlemen" or "Gentleman" as often as four times on a single page. Sometimes she uses the second person masculine as though face to face with one of the shaykhs. Had she been able to meet with Shaykh Muhammad Rahim al-Tarabulsi, for example, she would have told him he was wrong to claim that Islam cannot be compared with other religions and that its distinctiveness should be visually marked by the clothes men and women wear. No, she snapped, men should not follow their ancestors and wear turbans and long outer garments and women should not cover their faces in the streets and their heads and bosoms when at home. Did the learned Shaykh recommend a return to writing on parchment or palm leaves or stones and bones in emulation of the first recorders of the words of the Qur'an? If this is what he had in mind then he should bring even only the tiniest shred of evidence from the Qur'an or the Sunna. No, religions do not work like that; this insistence on religiously determined garments is mindless pursuit of tradition (*Unveiling and Veiling*, pp. 237–240).

The one and only Qur'anic verse that deals with covering refers not to hands and face but to the chest and breasts. If there is any consensus about covering it is the preference for uncovering that is derived from the fact that uncovered peasant women, who are more numerous than their veiled urban sisters, are not deemed bad Muslims. Above all, they are healthier because faces, hair and hands that are not exposed to sunlight sicken. As for Traditions calling for veiling they are probably invented and can be countered with others that call for unveiling (*Unveiling and Veiling*, pp. 248, 38).

Challenging Shaykh Mustafa al-Ghalayini, she wrote: "You mentioned, my dear Shaykh, that the health and morality of the Bedouin and the villagers earned them the right to be unveiled. It was the corrupt morality of city dwellers that blighted them with the veil. Excuse me, Sir, I am a village woman living in the city and I have observed both villagers and city dwellers. I have not seen your city sisters and brothers to be inherently less moral than my sisters and brothers from the villages. Indeed, the corruption appearing in the city is attributable to the corrupting influence of the face veil. Do you not see that life today necessitates unveiling? How is it that we do not permit the unveiling of the face when God forbad it to be covered during the Hajj and the Umra [the minor pilgrimage] when women are surrounded by many thousands of men and when so many women around the Prophet did not cover? How is it that we do not permit this when our minds have revealed to us how good it is to unveil and how bad it is to veil? Woe to us if we do not join with our men in breaking our chains to seize our freedoms that are gifts from God Almighty. They provide for the welfare, advancement and happiness of all" (*Unveiling and Veiling*, pp. 290–295, see also *The Girl and the Shaykhs*, p. 52).

If the function of the veil is to protect people from temptation, then hide all temptations! Let the rich hide from the poor their houses, clothes, food, and any kind of luxury. If the veil demarcates humans from animals then it is men, who think they are superior in reason, who must veil (*Unveiling and Veiling*, pp. 285–286).

Nazira was uncompromising in her call for the implementation of women's equality, real equality and not some vague notion of women's equal or even superior moral value. She challenged the specious notion of equal moral status that meant men and women were complementary to each other but with the caveat that men were in the public sphere and women in the private. Citing Qur'an 4:1, the verse about men and women being created simultaneously from a single soul, she asked the shaykhs, by what right "do you claim that you are by nature more perfect? Don't you know that girls are said to mature at age nine and boys only at twelve? Girls are subject to the laws of the Sharia three years before boys. In other words, women's reason is complete earlier than men's. Here are my proofs concerning the perfection of women's reason and religion, so bring on your proofs about their lack. The greatest Tradition claims that thinking for one hour is better than worshipping for 70 years." Another Tradition lauds daughters' emotional intelligence over that of sons: "There is no need to admonish you to love your daughters because they make themselves loveable through good deeds and their tenderness" (*Unveiling and Veiling*, pp. 102–105, 87–89, 94).

Since the Qur'an affirmed again and again that women were intellectually men's equals – and in two pages she listed fifteen verses about God distributing reason equally among humans so that all might see and act in accordance with the scriptures and revelations (*Unveiling and Veiling*, pp. 102–103) – where did these religious scholars get the idea of women's lack in reason and in religion? It was more than the reduction of women's value to half that of a man, because she had already understood that calculation. It was more than repudiation because it was not at all clear to her that men did have the unbridled right to dispose of their wives. As for polygyny, explained in Qur'an 4:3, it was clear that the extra wives a man might marry depended on his ability to practice absolute fairness among the wives – something that the same verse indicates is a problem and a later verse declares well nigh impossible. Moreover, polygyny like slavery should be abolished since it no longer served its original social function of providing protection for women who had lost their husbands in the many wars that had ravaged tribal society. From the Druze perspective the injunction to fairness among wives and its impossibility ruled out polygyny. She also mentioned approvingly Ataturk's decision to ban polygyny.

Nazira was convinced that it was the face veil that led to the opinion about women's lack of reason. It was the face veil that allowed men to say what they liked about women without attending to their responses. Because men could not see their faces they did not register women's reactions to their words. A voice muffled by cloth is inconsequential and easy to silence.

Above all, the veil enabled immoral behavior. Thieves cover their faces and so do prostitutes so that they will not be discovered. Why were the shaykhs so intent on covering women's faces? Were they trying to push women to commit crimes and sins? Or did the paralysis of half the population suit their purposes? After all, the paralyzed half is easy to ignore and forget (*Unveiling and Veiling*, pp. 100, 62).

In her research, Nazira came across many important men and particularly shaykhs like Muhammad 'Abduh who had written about the veil. The Egyptian judge Qasim Amin remained a reference among reformers calling for women's education and autonomy. "Is it not a disgrace," she quoted from Amin, "that we cannot imagine that our mothers, wives and sisters know how to protect themselves?" (*Unveiling and Veiling*, p.126).

She was withering in her attack on those opponents of unveiling who did not argue their case well. For example, Shaykh Muhammad Ibrahim al-Qayati al-Azhari, whose *The Sunna and the Book: a Judgment on Education and the Veil*, "was even more distorting than other texts and more oppressive to women ... no tyrant has been more unjust ... They have forbidden women all knowledge, even writing, and taught them to spin ... The black all-enveloping cloth and the face veil were not enough of a veil for them; they wanted the veils to be the walls of boudoirs to be left only for the grave ... The goal is to blind women's sight and insight" (*Unveiling and Veiling*, p. 227). How could Shaykh al-Qayati square his position with that of the Qur'an and the Traditions, of God and Muhammad, that all should seek knowledge even if it entailed traveling to China?

Agreeing with Aisha al-Taymuriya, Qasim Amin, and other Arab reformists, she declared that women's seclusion undermines a whole society so that it lags behind others that have included women in public space. No society can progress while its women are not respected and their rights are not protected. That is the universal message she framed in the particular language of the veil and the seclusion of women. The veil is not the sign of lack and inferiority, it is its instrument: "Some of us in this East have endured four kinds of darkness: the darkness of the cloth niqab (face veil), of the ignorance niqab, of the hypocrisy niqab, of the stagnation niqab" (*Unveiling and Veiling*, pp. 52, 59, 50). What was so outrageous was the reversal of blame; the ignorance, hypocrisy, and stagnation imposed on women were then attributed to them. Instead of acknowledging that the veil caused the ignorance, these shaykhs claimed that ignorance was inherent in women and that the veil mitigated it. In other words, it was only after the four veils had been layered one on top of another that women came to exemplify the ignorance that the veils represented and created. For Nazira, women are not deficient in reason and religion *before* covering their faces, only *afterwards*.

"Gentlemen, you accuse us of lack of religion and reason. Why? Because you have blocked the paths of the intellect and you have cast us into an ocean of humiliation and ignorance … Can there be religion where there is ignorance? The ignorant take from the surface of religion, and of what use is religion without its core?" (*Unveiling and Veiling*, p. 136).

Women, Nazira argued, are inherently rational and pious, never more so than when they uncover their faces. Stunting their intellectual capacities, the face veil prevents women from entering fully into the life of the community and contributing to it. Since it is the face veil that dehumanizes women, and it is men who impose it, then it is men who bear the responsibility for women's supposed deficiency in reason and religion.

The veil, in fact, was not for the common Muslim woman but rather for Muhammad's wives. Its purpose was to distinguish them and prevent them from being harassed. Later, it set the believers apart from slaves. Shaykh Hafidh al-Din al-Nasfi told a story about the second caliph 'Umar who punished a slave girl for wearing a veil and pretending to be free (*Unveiling and Veiling*, p. 171). But since slavery was a practice of the past, argued Nazira, the instrumental function of the veil no longer pertained. Clearly, she did not consider the four women, including the much beloved Zaynab, whom her parents had bought in Istanbul to be slaves.

Although many Druze women are *musattaha*, or covered with the white scarf wound around their head and then pulled under the nose and over the mouth, Nazira never covered her face because her family and especially her father and aunt Amira were opposed to any kind of veil. Until today, many Druze girls in the Chouf are *musattaha*.

Druze women

Nazira noted that neither Muslims nor non-Muslims looked
askance at her uncovered face, considering her modest attire sufficient to earn respect (*The Girl and the Shaykhs*, pp. 52, 130). As for
those shaykhs who claimed that Islam demanded that women cover
their faces, they should argue their case in court with those who
knew the law.

Had not Shaykh al-Ghalayini said that the veil was a holdover from
pre-Islamic culture and an accretion from the Byzantines and
Sassanians with whom the early Muslims associated as they radiated
out east and west from the Arabian Peninsula? For the Bedouin the
veil offered protection from the burning sun and whipping sand-
storms; for urban Persians and Byzantines the veil signaled class. A
man whose wife veiled was marked as elite because her veil and
seclusion precluded work.

Nazira found instances in early Islam of powerful, intellectual, and
highly regarded women meeting men without veils. The Prophet's
daughter Fatima al-Zahra' gave lectures and lessons to mixed audi-
ences her face uncovered. Writing about Muslim women leaders, she
quoted from *Scattered Pearls,* an 1894 compendium of famous
women's biographies by the Lebanese Zainab Fawwaz (1860–1914).
In the eleventh century,

> the highly respected Shaykha Shahda, known as Fakhr al-Nisa',
> lectured to elites in Baghdad mosques and schools about literature,
> history, and theology, and she was considered equal to the most
> respected religious authorities. Umm al-Khair and Umm Ibrahim
> taught students in Baghdad. Umm Sa'd bint 'Isam al-Sa'duna taught the
> science of Traditions and theology in the Cordoba madrasa.
> The medieval scholars Ibn Khallikan and Ibn Mas'ab wrote about
> Muhammad's beautiful granddaughter Sukayna, whose home became
> the Kaaba for people who came from all over the Muslim region to
> hear her lectures, and the great historian Ibn Khaldun had described
> how she had spoken to large mixed audiences. It is well known
> that Imam al-Shafii, founder of one of the four schools of Sunni
> jurisprudence, was instructed by Nafisa, the granddaughter of the
> fourth caliph 'Ali and thus the great granddaughter of the Prophet

Muhammad and also the wife of Ishaq b. Ja'far al-Sadiq. In the twelfth century, Ibn Athir, Ibn Jubayr, al-Mas'udi, al-Suyuti and al-Isfahani mentioned Khayzuran, who had encouraged her husband, the Abbasid caliph al-Mahdi, to build academies. She received scholars, poets, and rulers in their palace. Women during the caliphate of the Abbasids were empowered to do what later women could not. Zubayda, the wife of Harun al-Rashid, and his sister al-'Abbasa lectured to scholars. Qutr al-Nada, wife of Caliph al-Mu'tadid and mother of al-Muqtadir, attended all official gatherings. The fourteenth-century traveler Ibn Battuta wrote about Tatar women who summoned scholars and intellectuals at will.

(*Unveiling and Veiling*, pp. 274–276, 10, 160–161)

How could the shaykhs deny women positions of authority in Muslim societies when they had proved themselves to be capable leaders? By what right did they pronounce on women's rights when the only one to know what is right is God?

"If we rely on every turban we encounter, rather than deciding on what we have carefully deliberated, then we will extinguish our spiritual light with our own hands" (*Unveiling and Veiling*, p. 71). This kind of language was not calculated to please, but her purpose in writing this book was to provoke and not to please.

Assuming the role of a *mujtahida,* she re-interpreted the Qur'anic verse generally cited to insist that Muslim women stay at home and out of sight. Using traditional exegetical methodology, she argued against those who misinterpret a verse that is addressed only to the wives of the Prophet. The verse in question is "*wa qarna fi buyutikunna wa la tabarrajna tabarruja al-jahiliya al-ula*" (Qur'an 33:33 that is generally translated "and stay in your homes and do not make a display of your finery as women did during the age of ignorance preceding Islam"). The important word in this verse, the word men have used to authorize themselves to keep women at home, is *qarna*.

What God meant must be derived from the grammar of *qarna*. Was the first vowel an i or an a? Was it *qirna* or *qarna*? It is up to us women to consider the matter carefully when we make our decision. If it is *qirna* then it means that women must stay settled in their homes; if it is *qarna* then it refers to the way women should walk in their homes; they should tiptoe.

And the word, of course, was *qarna*. Nazira derived this interpretation from exegetes like 'Ala al-Din al-Sufi al-Khazin, 'Abdallah al-Nasfi, and Nasir al-Din al-Baidawi, thus anchoring her linguistic decision in widely accepted sources of Qur'anic exegesis. She then explained that the consensus surrounding the "a" in *qarna* must be taken seriously and she delves further into the various meanings of the three different roots. In a section entitled "*Qarna* is the imperative of *qaara* not *qarra*," she argues that of the three possible roots for *qarna,* the root was not *qarra* (to dwell) but *qaara* (to tiptoe) with a hint of *waqara* (to settle, to be dignified). Therefore, the meaning was not to stay in their houses, but rather indicated how they were to behave when at home: they were to tiptoe and also to conduct themselves with decorum. Moreover, this choice was not only grammatically correct, it also accorded with the common welfare, a key principle in scriptural hermeneutics. Imprisoning a woman in her home might be compared to the pre-Islamic practice of female infanticide.

Above all, it is well known that the verse did not implicate all women, only the women in the household of the Prophet who were the only ones for whom the second person feminine plural pronominal suffix –*kunna* (your) was reserved. Additionally, the preceding verse explicitly addresses the wives of the Prophet who "are not like any other women" and analogy with them is strictly forbidden (Qur'an 33:32). Just as *wa qarna fi buyutikunna* referred to Muhammad's wives only, so was it also they alone who were to be veiled because they were not like other Muslim women. Did not Muslim women after hearing these verses ask why there were no specific verses referring to them? And al-Nasfi had responded that ordinary Muslim women were addressed only when the words *Muslimat* (Muslim women) or *mu'minat* (believing women) appeared in the verse.

In challenging a widely accepted interpretation of a misogynist verse, Nazira provided a model of how women should use their minds in order to understand what the verses related to women mean. Each woman is responsible for her own interpretations and behavioral decisions. "What I have just discussed is a linguistic matter that concerns our living conditions; it is our right to comment on it, to try to understand it. Moreover, we have the indisputable right to make others understand."

She is absolutely convinced of the correctness of her interpretation, saying that the Qur'an contains knowledge that will correct the mistakes of scholars across time. She proposed the formation of a high-level committee of progressive Islamic authorities to revise all extant interpretations in light of their understanding of God's Book (*Unveiling and Veiling*, pp. 154–158, 146, 162–164, 173–174). In *The Girl and the Shaykhs* she expands at length on her interpretation of the controversial word *qarna* (*The Girl and the Shaykhs*, pp. 345–352, 358–365).

Her closing words, that some supporters would later repeat, invoked Abu Hanifa, one of the founding fathers of Islamic law: were he to be resurrected, along with other leading jurists, and to see the world in its current condition he would call for the removal of the veil (*The Girl and the Shaykhs*, p. 184).

Nazira and her father distributed copies of *Unveiling and Veiling* far and wide, using the network of Lebanese emigrants scattered around the world, and especially in the Americas. Letters poured in, and the book was reviewed in major journals and newspapers around the world. Some loved it; some hated it. In April 1928, the Syrian prime minister Taj al-Din al-Hasani wrote her a note in which he thanked her for sending him this "unique and precious gift that I will cherish as the best reminder of your grace, literary skill and praiseworthy effort expended on behalf of the progress of women."

Ahmad Nami Bey, the former Syrian president, visited the Karakol Druze house to congratulate the author in person (Bu Matar 2008, p. 169). A little later, Shaykh 'Abd al-Qadir al-Maghribi published a letter in *Al-Ahrar* #959 admiring her grasp of the Qur'an and Traditions: "It is as though she had said: 'My Druze religion, despite its historical traditions that distinguish it from other branches of

رئيس الوزارة

حضرة الآنسة الاديبة الفاضلة
تحية واحترام . تناولت كتابك الكريم ومعه مؤلفك القيم في السفور
والحجاب الذى خطه يراعك البليغ فاشكر لك هذه الهدية النفيسة
النادرة التي ساحتفظ بها كاحسن ذكرى لفضلك وادبك وسعيك
المشكور لترقية المرأة. والسلام مختوم باحترام لفضلك وادبك ايتها
الآنسة المحترمة .
دمشق ٢٥ نيسان ٩٣٨

Letter from Syrian prime minister, Taj al-Din al-Hasani

Islam, holds to the firm tie of Islam and is guided by it.'" It did not
matter to this shaykh that the author of this polemical tract engaging
with some central issues of Islam and Islamic law was not a Sunni
Muslim without the necessary credentials from Islamic institutions
to be authorized to interpret scripture.

The Syrian education minister Muhammad Bey Kurd 'Ali wrote
in *Al-Baraq* #3011 that Miss Zeineddine had succeeded where others
before her had failed. He liked the book so much that he asked her to
send twenty copies to the Arab Science Academy. Shortly after being
fired from al-Azhar in 1925 "for arguing that Islam leaves the form of
government to human invention" (Kurzman 1998, p. 11), the liberal
Egyptian Shaykh 'Ali 'Abd al-Raziq (1888–1966) published a review
in *Al-Hilal*. He expressed surprise that the controversy surrounding

unveiling was still urgent in Lebanon when it was no longer an issue in Egypt, where the veil seemed to have become a thing of the past for his compatriots (*The Girl and the Shaykhs*, pp. 147, 143–144, 150–152).

Especially vivid were the several interviews Nazira gave at home with her father often in attendance. Fawzi al-Rifai, editor of the Aleppo paper *Al-Nahda al-Halabiya*, described his sense of awe while waiting in the parlor for Nazira. When she arrived, tall and elegant with a scarf tied attractively around her hair, she welcomed him warmly.

"How are my sisters in Aleppo faring?"

"Not too well." Some were locked in their homes, where they were treated like slaves and beaten, others were veiled but could move about freely and "only a few were completely free and modestly unveiled."

"What harm would there be, if all women could leave their home unveiled to partake of the freedom God gave them and men denied them?"

No, she did not want to publish a journal in which she might make her ideas more widely known because she was completing requirements for her second Baccalaureate in philosophy. The reference to the Baccalaureate was a reminder of her youth.

"What do you think about the law that Ataturk promulgated concerning men and women's equality of witness?" The Turkish government had just overturned the Islamic law concerning women's witness being worth only half a man's witness. No longer would courts have to bring two women for every man summoned to testify.

"There's nothing new in it," she declared categorically. But even if it was not new, the reform in witness laws had implications for inheritance that was no longer half for women but a full share. Rifai closed the interview with a comment to the reader about Nazira's maturity, erudition, and elegant Arabic that he urged Syrian women to emulate (*The Girl and the Shaykhs*, pp.128–131).

In a subsequent interview with *Al-Raya*, she compared the shaykhs with a man in Istanbul who was to give a sermon on the tenth of

Muharram to a congregation of Iranian Shiites. The worshipers thought he was going to talk about the murder of Husayn, the grandson of the Prophet Muhammad, because his death is annually commemorated on the tenth of Muharram with extravagant lamentations. No sooner had he opened his mouth than the people started to wail and beat their breasts. They did not hear a word of his sermon that did not even touch on the topic of Karbala and Husayn. Hopefully, readers would not do the same with her book. "We all smiled – I, Nazira, and her father – at this apt comparison."

"What do you mean by unveiling?" the reporter asked.

"I mean uncovering the face because it is the site of women's feelings, revealing their soul. Look at a woman's face and you will encounter her intellect, her reason and the most important aspects of her life. I have expressly condemned any kind of nakedness or inappropriate behavior like ballroom dancing, un-chaperoned meetings between men and women and anything that does not enhance women's morals."

Was she going to rebut some of the critiques? "I published my book so that it might speak to the Arab nation. For the time being, I will be silent and let men and women speak. Then, and only if necessary, will I speak."

In conclusion, he asked her if she thought the opposition to her book would last. "Yes," she replied optimistically, "but not for long" (*The Girl and the Shaykhs*, pp. 120–122).

A reporter from *Al-Hurriya* asked if she was going to respond to the shaykhs and this time she was more caustic: "So far no one has come up with anything better or provided a more persuasive proof that I should bother to speak."

The interviewer wondered how someone who had studied only in foreign schools could be so versed in Islam. Annoyed, she repeated to him the story she assumed he had read on pages 55–56 – note the precision – about Shaykh al-Faqih who had told her that she should not make any pronouncements about Islam until she had absorbed the basic texts that he recommended. She went on to describe how her father had then taken full responsibility for her Islamic education. When the interviewer asked what she thought of those who called her an unbeliever, her answer was vintage Nazira.

"The noble Tradition teaches us that 'Whoever calls a believer an unbeliever is an unbeliever.' History teaches us that it is an ancient custom for all reformers, including saints and prophets, to be accused of unbelief. The people first charge with unbelief but then they venerate ... whoever charges a believer with disbelief is indeed an infidel" (*The Girl and the Shaykhs*, pp.123–124, 225).

Clearly, she expected ultimately to find favor when the people had seen the errors of the ways of the shaykhs and the maliciousness of their complaints. So convinced was she that her message was prophetic that she even compared herself with Jesus Christ and Muhammad who had been opposed in their lifetimes but whose light shone on after them (*The Girl and the Shaykhs*, p. 97). It was this kind of brashness that repelled many of her male readers; they must have frowned on a young woman throwing herself into the field of polemics they thought to be their preserve. But Nabulsi was impressed and he encouraged his women readers to be as courageous and honest as Miss Nazira: "It is your responsibility, Ladies, to bring the current awakening to fruition" (*The Girl and the Shaykhs*, pp. 125–128).

On 15 October 1928, while attending the steering committee meeting of the International Feminist Organization in Berlin, Huda Shaarawi wrote to Nazira: "I have received your lovely gift of *Unveiling and Veiling* and I thank you for this impassioned cry for the liberation of women ... Our sex is honored and made proud by the likes of you" (*The Girl and the Shaykhs*, pp. 165–169).

Among the luminaries of the day who congratulated her was no less than the Egyptian king Fu'ad. In 1929 he sent her a poem entitled "The Voice of Truth," addressed to the Joan of Arc of the East and scripted by a calligrapher, the lawyer Najib Hawawini. In this poem he played with the meaning of her family name Zeineddine, Arabic for 'Adornment of Religion':

Young woman, you carried the banner of your jihad
To remove from religion what others had attached to it

The facts in your case have been corroborated
And the world has been adorned with the adornment of religion
You have become the Joan of Arc of the East
Indeed you have outdone Joan with your determination and certainty
Their Joan of Arc destroyed the walls of the Bastille
Made of stones large and small and of clay
You have destroyed superstitions
Mighty as mountains
Future generations will venerate you
When reason will have guided this poor East of ours.

(The Girl and the Shaykhs, p. 246)

The reference to the fifteenth-century French Catholic woman warrior echoed the interest in Joan of Arc that Egyptian and Lebanese feminists had been expressing in their journals since the late

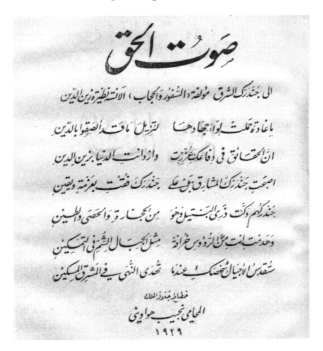

Poem from King Fu'ad, "The Voice of Truth" (courtesy of Said Zeineddine)

nineteenth century. But the applause merely fanned the flames of opponents' ire. The negative responses among the opponents of unveiling soon turned vicious. Fanatics roamed around town nailing warnings on the doors of proponents of unveiling. Like notices of demolition, they let the occupants of the house know that if they, meaning the men in particular, did not cease their activities against the veil they would suffer the consequences.

Nazira's greatest shock and lesson came from her dealings with the Mufti who had promised to be her ally. On 12 April 1928, she sent him a copy of *Unveiling and Veiling* with a long letter that she published in *Al-Ahrar*. Confident of his approval of her scholarship, she wanted to draw his and others' attention to the key points she was making. Most important was the question of knowledge and Muhammad's insistence that all believers seek knowledge even if it meant traveling to China. Like the light of the sun, the light of knowledge shines on everyone. She wanted the Mufti and others to know that it was her intimate knowledge of convent schools and French colleges that had intensified her commitment to Islam. Ironically, it was there, of all places, that she had learned that Islam gives women more rights than any other religion. No religious law, however, had been more unjust to women than the shaykhs' law.

Did not the Prophet say that reason is human religion, and human religion will not be complete until reason is complete? Didn't the Sufi Shaykh Muhyi al-Din Ibn 'Arabi say that Muslims should take guidance directly from God, and not from people who rely on tradition and repetition? She hoped the Mufti would approve of her book. Should he find anything truly wrong then she would write another book (*The Girl and the Shaykhs*, pp. 114–119). In return for the book, the Mufti sent her a signed poem of praise in his own elegant hand!

Nazira's satisfaction was short-lived. In the brouhaha that broke out after the publication of the book, the Mufti scrambled to cover his back. To her shock, he published "Legality of the Veil," a refutation in a publication entitled *Al-Ahd al-Jadid* (#466) in which he mounted a strong defense of the face veil, calling unveiling a disease that only the stupid and the accursed demand when the time is not right

(*The Girl and the Shaykhs*, p. 69). Nazira shot back in the interview with *Minerva*'s 'Abd al-Salam Nabulsi, exposing the Mufti's contradictory response to her book; he had even quoted from a poem she had quoted on p. 276 – note her meticulous referencing!

Had his objections persuaded her to change anything? No, he merely confirmed that the veil might be removed in a time that is not corrupt (*The Girl and the Shaykhs*, pp. 125–127). How could he, of all people, someone she had consulted, condemn the book publicly after privately praising it!

6

"THE GIRL" WRITES BACK

In July 1928, a mere four months after the publication of *Unveiling and Veiling*, Shaykh al-Ghalayini published a book-length refutation entitled *Views on the Book "Attributed to Miss Nazira Zeineddine."* The key word is "attributed." As though trying to mitigate the vehemence of his criticism, he claimed that it was not Miss Nazira who had written the book but rather a team of men. She had asked his opinion, and he gave it in a book filled with condescension and spite.

The family was in Ayn Qani for the summer and the postman had just delivered the mail with the almost daily letter for Miss Nazira Zeineddine from some distant place. That day's delivery included a copy of the Shaykh's book. Said Bey took it to his room off the terrace, sat down with a glass of arak and a plate of olives, and skimmed it from cover to cover.

"Well, Nazira, it looks as though you were right about Shaykh al-Ghalayini. This is a travesty. The book is a full-scale attack on yours. Well, he is confused about this. He does not know whom to attack because he's trying to claim you aren't the author."

That evening after dinner, Said Bey assembled the family in the living area so they could all listen to what Shaykh al-Ghalayini had written about Nazira and the book. Every night after Kamil went to bed, they would gather to discuss the events of the day, and the recent international reactions to the book. Munir was getting tired of the incessant attention lavished on his sister, but his father insisted that he stay, telling him that when he joined the army, he would be free of this tiresome obligation.

Hala, Munira, and Munir joined Nazira and her father in the living room. He chuckled while reading: " 'I knew that a Sunni and a Shiite, a Christian and a faithless Christian and Muslim and a teacher and a lawyer and a missionary had all collaborated in writing this book.' But then he adds patronizingly, 'We don't want to believe this to be the case.' The rest of the book refers interchangeably to you, Nazira, and to the writers, always in the third person masculine plural [al-Ghalayini 1928, pp. 1, 2, 14–17].

"He's connected the publication of the book with a recently concluded conference of missionaries in Jerusalem. He claims that these infidels deluded you and me."

"Why you? I thought Nazira had written the book," Hala asked.

"Of course, she did. He is protecting himself against allegations he's attacking a colleague by claiming that we allowed ourselves to be party to this deception."

"So," Nazira smiled, "we are both gullible fools taken in by wicked frauds. Wasn't that what people said about Qasim Amin after he published *The Liberation of Women?*"

"That's right. Some people even claimed that Lord Cromer had urged him to write it. How ridiculous those critics now seem, and yet we seem to be seeing the same thing today, don't we? But I suspect that this is going to backfire. He's so angry he doesn't see how he is incriminating himself. Our elegant Shaykh with his neat little mustache and clean-shaven chin has lashed out against the section about facial hair."

"Why did you write about mustaches and beards?" Munira was puzzled.

"Because these religious authorities claim to be following the Sunna of the Prophet, but they flagrantly disobey his example."

Nazira opened her book at the offending page: "How impoverished is the nation in which only half the population is rational and therefore able to participate fully in its political and spiritual life. How impoverished is the man whose mother, wife, sister, and daughter are said to be lacking! The problem is that from the beginning men established laws that contravene God's dictates for Muslims.

They permitted the forbidden and forbad the permitted. They built statues when creating anything in God's image is known to be idolatry. They allowed the drinking of alcohol when it is clearly forbidden. They let their moustaches grow when the Sunna demanded they be clipped and they cut their beards when normative practice was to let them grow. They should let their beards grow and trim their moustaches and not dare to claim it is God's will that women's faces be covered when there is no mention of such covering in the scriptures" (*Unveiling and Veiling*, pp. 77–82, 86).

Munir whistled quietly. Stroking his soft mustache, he asked his sister whether she had not gone overboard with this generalization about all men. Proud of the latest proof of his manhood, he pointed to his top lip proudly.

"I wanted to discuss the problem of hypocrisy and facial hair was only part of a longer list of men's deviations from orthodoxy. Why did he pick up on this passage?"

"He's taken your generalization so seriously that he's fallen into a trap of his own making," Said Bey was amused as he read aloud: " 'As for mustaches, young Lady, many have shaved them.' I wonder if he's talking about himself."

Everyone laughed. They would be certain to check with friends who were still in Beirut as to whether the dandy now sported a beard and no mustache.

" 'Leave our beards and mustaches alone and occupy yourself with your forelocks and side locks and short haircuts. Religion is more important than this trivia.' He then categorically refuses your demand that women be acknowledged as men's equals in mind and status. He is not happy!" [al-Ghalayini 1928, pp. 35–39]

"If hair is so trivial why has he written so much about it?" Hala asked timidly.

"He must have felt threatened," Said Bey mused.

"Well, let him bring proof that I am wrong. He knows he can't. I wanted to point out how inconsistent he is about religious mandates for how men and women should and should not deal with hair. I will be satisfied if each breath that men and women take when they make their decisions about their hair is free. If he agrees to the proposition that men and women have the legal right to choose, then our disagreement is over and Muslim men and women can call a truce. If not, he is an unjust tyrant" (*The Girl and the Shaykhs*, p. 380).

They were taken aback by the tone of the book, especially since al-Ghalayini was a respected shaykh who would not be expected to descend to such language.

"Listen to page 33," Said Bey said, "he seems to think that you should not have taken a position about the veil even though he knows that what you have written is no more radical than Qasim Amin's argument against the veil made thirty years ago in *Liberation of Women*. The ink must have splattered all over the paper as he spat out 'Who gave you the idea that you could speak for the opponents of the veil? You have no right to speak on behalf of Muslim women as a whole.'

"In a chapter summarizing the mistakes, he waxes lyrical about you (or about the many writers? Since he continuously shifts between Miss Nazira and the unspecified men, it is hard to know whom he is blaming). You, or they, he writes, have claimed that men have no reason, or that they are deficient in reason, or that women are more rational than men. They (here he is referring to multiple authors) 'became very confused in this matter. And they affirmed that Miss Zeineddine is the most knowledgeable and that the shaykhs in the past and the present are ignorant, stupid, deceitful, hypocritical, and that she alone (may God bless and forgive her) was able to assume the throne of knowledge and understanding and to interpret the Qur'anic verses, especially those connected with the veil and women' [see al-Ghalayini 1928, p. 21]. My goodness, where did you write that? Did I miss something?"

"Of course not. You wouldn't have let me get away with such hubris. But I do believe that a woman is more qualified to interpret verses that deal with women's rights and duties because it is she who is being addressed."

Shaykh al-Ghalayini had done his utmost to discredit Nazira. He was citing her arguments in out-of-context fragments and, despite his assertion that she was not the author, it was Nazira that he pilloried. She was not sure whether to be angry or flattered that someone so well known had taken the trouble to write an entire book about hers.

"He claims on page 32 that after reading the reactions of so many who had not even read the book he felt compelled to set the record straight. Furthermore, his colleagues had pushed him to go public with his views."

"Is that why he preached about the book in the Majidiya Mosque three weeks in a row?" Munira asked.

"He should let me stand next to him when he shouts out his lies so that I could show the people how wrong he is. If he cannot provide proof that others wrote the book, and needless to say he can't, he should just keep silent."

"But he won't keep silent because, as he writes, he took the pulpit each Friday to correct the many mistakes and to make sure that the public not be led astray. He is incensed that you openly enlisted the help of the French."

For the first and only time Nazira seemed a little unsure of herself: "Would it have been better not to publish my letter to Ponsot? Since it was the French authorities in Syria, under pressure from the shaykhs, who had persuaded the government to forbid Muslim women from leaving the house unveiled, it was to them that I had to direct my protest."

On 3 April 1928, Nazira had sent the French High Commissioner, a certain Henri Ponsot (1877–1963), ten copies of *Unveiling and Veiling*. In the accompanying letter she enlisted his help in assuring the shaykhs that the veil was a social and not a religious matter. Since their mandate did not allow them to interfere in religious matters they could have no say in the veil controversy. Far from covering up her appeal to the French Mandate authorities, she sent a copy of this letter to *Lisan al-Hal,* and nine days later the newspaper published it with a glowing introduction.

It is worth dwelling briefly on this letter to the French high commissioner because it reveals Nazira's attitude and relationship to the French, her criticism of the shaykhs, and her belief in an Islam that guarantees freedom for all, especially in matters of religious interpretation. She began with praise for Western civilization – except for "abominations" like women's indecent exposure and ball-room dancing. She deplored the backwardness of Muslim societies in which women veil. Almost as though advertising the book, she summarized its contents: Islam is not opposed to women mixing with men; women are rational human beings who should be educated in order to participate in the political life of their communities; social reform is impossible if part of the society is not active; women and men should engage equally and rationally with their religion; Muslims should not follow human but rather God's law, and they should bind themselves to the Qur'an that calls for dress appropriate to time and place; Muslims should establish brotherly relations with Christians according to the teachings of Jesus and Muhammad; Muslims must take wisdom from wherever they can find it, including the West. She concluded with a plea to the French not to interfere in matters of religion but to support "poor Muslim women who have been treated in a way that contradicts the Book of God, the Sunna of his Prophet, the rule of reason and the norms of society." Signing off, she assured Ponsot of her belief that her book would serve her country and countrywomen but also fulfill another, very problematic, goal: facilitate the task of the Mandate in its reform efforts. To that end, she asked him to police the aggressions perpe-trated against the defenders of unveiling (*The Girl and the Shaykhs*, pp. 110–114).

"Yes," Said Bey mused, "that was probably not a wise move. When talking about your connections to the French, al-Ghalayini no longer refers to the male writers of the book but to Miss Nazira Zeineddine. He cites specific pages that he characterizes as full of deviance, vul-garity, and ugliness. But then, lest he offend, he concedes, 'All that this young lady knows about this book is that her name decorates the cover.' Only to end up with the ultimate insult: 'I do not believe that anyone will acknowledge any kind of excellence in her, for she is an ordinary, naïve girl with a deficient education.'

"That's rich! He knows that you have had the best education available to girls in the region. He's faulted you (or is it them?) for citing too many irrelevant Qur'anic verses and Traditions about human freedom that ended up in chaos. For him, reason is not the only judge in matters of religion because few can understand religion without some guidance" [see al-Ghalayini 1928, pp. 32, 22, 59, 120].

It was late. Her siblings had gone to the roof to sleep, but Hala stayed up with her husband and daughter. She sensed trouble ahead.

"Why is he so mean-spirited?" Hala was upset.

"Oh Mother, didn't you notice he's pretending I'm not the author! It's as though he were my father or tutor and I a bit of an idiot!"

"Do you know why he's written the book?" Said Bey asked rhetorically. "He's peeved. In the conclusion he complains that 'Nazira Zeineddine,' note that it is you again who is the author, 'had devoted thirty-eight pages in which they,' note the change back to the third person masculine plural pronoun, 'refuted some parts of our book *Islam the Soul of Civilization or Islam and Lord Cromer* that was published twenty years ago in 1908'."

All three burst into laughter. Nazira reminded her parents of her encounter with the Shaykh months earlier and how Said Bey had tried to convince her that al-Ghalayini was supportive of women and the only problem with him and his book was that he was a bit out of date. Said Bey nodded.

"Well, that is the very same excuse that he uses today: 'We wrote this book when we were very young but it remains the work of reference on the subject.' In the very next paragraph he writes that the authors, no longer you, Nazira, 'want to take women out of the home and thus destroy her natural disposition. We do not want this to happen.' I suppose this is his way to prove that he is not trying to mount a self-defense but only, and I quote, 'to correct the lies and misguided interpretations and to reveal what *their* ignorance has led them to do.'

"Here you are again in the very next paragraph; he is thanking you for having noted what he wrote about women 'because I am and always will be an advocate for women, working for their advancement. But I disagree with the authors (plural!) of your book in many respects because what they are advocating will corrupt Muslim women and what we want is to reform their situation through the kinds of knowledge and religion that are suitable for their nature'."

Snatching the book out of her father's hands, she read out loud.

"'Before finishing this book, we will say a word of truth about this young lady. She is naïve, polite, good, and noble. She is far from being vulgar or showy. But she has allowed herself to be duped by these writers. Maybe once she has learned the truth she will return to the right path and then do her best to advance the cause of Muslim women through knowledge and religion,' as he has! 'Because God does not lead astray those who seek to do good' [al-Ghalayini 1928, pp. 191–194].

"This is vintage al-Ghalayini. So nice about me, deluded as I am, but what a son of a bitch about women."

"Control your tongue!" Hala snapped uncharacteristically.

"Sorry, Mother, but you need to read some of the outrageous things he has written about women, and clearly about me. He's even stooped to insulting my looks!"

"Really? Why have your father and I already received proposals for your hand in marriage?" Nazira, however, was too busy trying to find something that she did not react.

"Where was it? Ah yes, here it is, page 129: 'Poor women, you whom God has not blessed with beauty, you are zero in the sight of men. Thank God that you must not be seen, lest we have to avert our eyes from you. Do not take revenge on Miss Nazira for she is one of you!' What do you think? How weak is the Shaykh's spirit!" (*The Girl and the Shaykhs*, pp. 384).

In his analysis of the Zeineddine affair over half a century later, Nabil Bu Matar criticizes Shaykh al-Ghalayini's tone and style. Referring readers to al-Ghalayini's *Views,* pp. 102ff., 32, 47, 66, and 74, he describes the Shaykh's "fanatical opposition to women whom he arrogantly accuses of deficient religion and reason and inferiority to men. He denounces facts about the ignorance of some Muslim scholars, exegetes and jurists when it is Nazira who alludes to them, even though he himself has cited these very same facts" (Bu Matar 2008, pp. 185–186).

Nazira learned later that al-Ghalayini had confided to some colleagues that he would not have opposed Nazira had she not opposed him in her book. But for that opposition he would have "raised the banner of her noble cause and joined her, but she insulted me and excluded me" (*The Girl and the Shaykhs*, p. 383). And in *Views* he mentions her critique with considerable annoyance, "all we wanted was that women's freedom should be fair and connected to what suits their nature and upbringing." Moreover, he accused her (or is it them?) of unjustly criticizing him for contradicting himself, and his humiliating commentary went so far as to try to justify himself, saying: "The research on the Muslim women in our book was of the highest caliber. Indeed, it was reprinted in Egypt in 1926" (al-Ghalayini 1928, pp. 24, 25).

Miss Nazira was not one to keep quiet and polite with such provocation. Within less than a year, she published a sizzling sequel entitled *The Girl and the Shaykhs: Views and Debates about "Unveiling and Veiling" and the Liberation of the Intellect and the Liberation of Women and Social Renewal in the Islamic World* (1929). Note the addition of the "Liberation of the Intellect" that she has added to the subtitle of the first volume. She is determined that her argument concerning the intellectual equality of women and men be highlighted. This book contained extracts from the numerous reactions and reviews, with her fearless rebuttals and over two hundred pages of praise from Lebanon, Syria, Egypt, Brazil, Argentina, New York, Venezuela, Mexico, and Iraq. Veteran feminist poets like the Iraqis Jamil Sidqi al-Zahawi (1863–1936) and Ma'ruf al-Rusafi (1875–1945) praised the author and exhorted young women to uncover their faces (*The Girl and the Shaykhs*, pp. 101–106). An Argentine journalist regretted that he was not on the Nobel Prize committee to be able to nominate her.

Many agreed with her when she wrote: "My book is the first of its kind to raise such thoughts, so do not prevent the people from hearing this invitation to an awakening. Their night has been long so let

تحرير: خالد البسام

نسوان زمان

صفحـات تهتم
بأخبـار وأحـوال
المرأة أيـام زمـان

الممثل المصري محسن سرحان يجيب عن سؤال مهم:
ماذا يريد الرجل من المرأة؟

حبيبة وأم وطباخة وجميلة وفنانة وكريمة

القاهرة ـ في ٢١ أغسطس (آب) ١٩٥٢:

هل أنت المرأة التي تحقق لزوجها كل ما يريده منها؟ طبعاً هذا أصعب سؤال لأية امرأة في الدنيا. غير أن المرأة الذكية تستطيع أن تحقق أغلب ما يريده الرجل كي يشعر بالسعادة معها.

حول هذا السؤال المهم لأية امرأة يجيب الممثل المعروف محسن سرحان في حديث صحافي نشر له في القاهرة أمس ويذكر فيه ماذا يريد الرجل بالضبط من المرأة. فيقول الممثل سرحان:

* يريد الرجل أن تكون زوجته هي حبيبته، أي انه يريد أن تكون عواطفها نحوه، كما كانت يوم لقاءها أول مرة وتقاسمها في الزواج. فهو يطلب منها أن تحدثه دائماً عن حبها له وتشعره بأن الحياة الزوجية لا تقوم إلا على الحب والوفاء.

* ويريدها صديقته وزميلته، فأن الصداقة يمكن أن تمتزج بالحب، فإذا أصبح الزوجان صديقين على مر السنين، فقد حققا حقاً السعادة المثالية، كما أن الزوج يستطيع أن يقضي بصحبتها أوقات فراغه بدلاً من أن يفرع إلى المقاهي باحثاً عن صديق يؤنس وحدته ويتحدث إليه.

* ويريدها ذات شخصية تعرف كيف تستلفت انظار الناس وتكسب إعجابهم بثقافتها وسعة اطلاعها وطريقتها في الحديث، أي انه يريدها سيدة في مجتمع فاضلة.

* ويريدها «أماً» تتفانى في حب أولادها، وتعرف كيف تربيهم، وتوجههم في الطريق المستقيم، وتسوسهم وتحميهم من آلامهم.

* ويريدها ربة بيت تعرف كيف تخلق من الفسيح شريات، أي أن تفعل المعجزات لتعيش بايدار زوجها المحدود دون أن

يشعر بنقص في بيته، وأن تكون راعية لهذا البيت ساهرة على شؤونه.

* ويريدها طباخة ماهرة تحذق فن الطهو وتبتكر في ألوان الطعام، فإن طبقاً من الطعام الشهي قد يكون له أثر في قلب الرجل أكثر من كلمة طريقة من الزوجة.

* ويريدها جميلة تعرف كيف تبدو في سن العشرين مهما تقدمت بها السن. فكثير من السيدات يهملن أنفسهن يعد أن يرزقن بأولاد، ويصبحن حياة مسؤولة على حساب جمالهن ورشاقتهن.

* ويريدها فنانة تتذوق الفن والجمال، وتعرف كيف تخلق من بيتها فردوسا يعود إليه الزوج فيتسى فيه متاعب الحياة والكفاح من أجل الرزق.

* ويريدها خفيفة الدم بارعة النكتة، لا يعرف وجهها العبوس والتجهم، تبتسم وتضحك دائماً.

* ويريدها هادئة الطبع لا تثور ولا تغضب لأتفه الأسباب، وإذا غضب هو قابلت غضبه بهدوء وابتسامة لطيفة تعيد إليه هدوءه وتزيل عنه أسباب الغضب.

* ويريدها كريمة، ولكن في الحد المعقول، فلا تسرف في الكرم، أو تغل يدها كل منها فتكون هي وزوجها موضع السخرية.

* ويريدها طيبة القلب، تكره الشر ولا تفعل إلا كل ما يرضي ضميرها، محبة لعمل الخير.. ولكن ذكية مهذبة، سليمة التفكير.

هذا جل ما يريده الرجل في المرأة، إن لم يكن كله، وهو أكثر من الكثير. وقلما يتوافر في امرأة واحدة. والسعيدة من فازت برجل قنوع تكفيه بعض هذه الصفات و«يصمص» عن الباقي.

الصورة: الممثل محسن سرحان

الأديبة نظيرة زين الدين

كتاب أديبة لبنانية شابة عن نهضة المرأة يثير ضجة في العالم العربي

بيروت في ٢ ديسمبر (كانون الأول) ١٩٢٩:

قامت أديبة لبنانية شابة بتأليف كتاب عن النهضة النسائية العربية بعنوان «السفور والحجاب». وقد أحدث الكتاب الذي قامت بتأليفه الآنسة نظيرة زين الدين ردود أفعال كبيرة في العالم العربي اتسم معظمها بالتأييد لأفكارها وآرائها في دور المرأة وحقوقها ومستقبلها. وبسبب هذه الردود وحماستها في التأليف أصدرت الأديبة اللبنانية نظيرة زين الدين كتاباً جديداً طرح في الأسواق قبل أيام بعنوان «الفتاة والشيوخ» ضمنته أقوال أهل الفضل والعلم في كتابها الأول وردودا مفحمة على منتقديها لمؤلفها الأول. وتضمن أيضاً آراء جريئة على خصوم نهضة وتقدم المرأة العربية.

Review of *The Girl and the Shaykhs*

the day begin" (*The Girl and the Shaykhs*, p. 87). She wanted her book to herald the dawn of reason and correct interpretation of scripture.

Having dedicated the first book to her father, Nazira dedicated this one to women in general, saying how happy she had been while writing *Unveiling and Veiling* because she had thought she was serving the best interests of Muslims and the Arab-Muslim nation. Concerned to show what was positive in Islam, she had been disappointed to learn that "my *umma* is not pleased with its girl." Always tongue in cheek, she added, "and yet I took the Qur'an and Sunna as my guide so perhaps the *umma* is not pleased with them" (*The Girl and the Shaykhs*, pp. 11–12).

Angry with those whose views on women and gender she had commended in her book but who had attacked her, she mocked the hypocrisy of former fans who were attempting to distance themselves from the controversy. Were they not aware of the damage they were doing to their society? She was scathing: "When writing my book I consulted their letters and published books ... I saw from them nothing but approval and heard nothing but thanks ... Is it appropriate to attribute ill will to someone who had shown shaykhs and scholars her book while it was being written and before it was printed in order to be sure it was correct? Isn't it possible to consider those who approved some parts of her book and who then thanked her to be participants in the work?" (*The Girl and the Shaykhs*, p. 93). As we know, this was no mere rhetoric. How could she trust the Mufti or any of the shaykhs who had first praised and then betrayed?

She vowed she would not show any of them the current book and if there were mistakes or problems this time it would be their fault because they had proven themselves treacherous (*The Girl and the Shaykhs*, pp. 91–95). Having shown respect for their learning, she could not understand why they were dismissive. As she had written in *Unveiling and Veiling,* "it is fine to disagree but we must respect each other's differences because one of us might be right" (*Unveiling and Veiling*, p. 61). Yet on 23 November she did send some, the Mufti included, a copy of *The Girl and the Shaykhs,* asking him to re-read the first book. On 6 December, he repeated that each must follow his own muse.

Her language became militaristic; she was conducting a *jihad,* and "her book provided them with some new weapons with which to find the truth." Moreover, referring to King Fu'ad's poem, she wrote that it was as though the soul of Joan of Arc had transmigrated into her —

note the rare reference to the Druze belief in metempsychosis (*The Girl and the Shaykhs*, pp. 14, 17, 99). The Druzes believe that upon the death of a Druze her soul is reincarnated in the body of a newborn Druze. Of course, Nazira was speaking metaphorically since Joan of Arc was not a Druze and her soul would have had to pass through many generations to reach Nazira's body.

Nor was the militaristic intent of her revolution lost on readers. One called the book a "battle against the Muslim woman's veil. The brilliant writer used all kinds of weapons to fight it. *Unveiling and Veiling* contains a cannonball shot at the army of darkness, the army of backwardness, and she will have a huge influence on the leadership of that army." Another added: "You did not bring new weapons; rather you fought them with their own weapons." Several called her a *mujahida* (*The Girl and the Shaykhs*, pp. 217, 234–237).

The second half of the book is addressed to religious authorities, whom she may address several times in a single page as "Gentlemen Opponents" or "Honorable Arrow Slingers." With wild abandon she takes on the shaykhs one by one. How could Shaykh Salah al-Din think he could get away with citing a false Tradition, or Shaykh Said al-Jabi claim she had twisted the Tradition about women lacking in reason and religion and stubbornly repeat that because women are lacking they should not be educated? How could Shaykh Salim Hamdan claim that "lapses in men's chastity do not impact their honor in the way that they do in women whether women like it or not. Loss of honor in women throws a burning ember into the heart"? She ridiculed his pseudo-scientific disquisition about the size of women's brains – apparently, women's brains are 1,155 grams lighter than men's – and the relationship of brain size to intelligence. That must mean that bulls and elephants are the most rational of all God's creatures (*The Girl and the Shaykhs*, pp. 37–38, 43). Her argument echoes the 1887 physical versus mental strength debate waged between Shibli Shumayyil (1850–1917) and various women on the pages of the *Al-Muqtataf* journal (Zachs & Halevi 2009, pp. 623–624).

And, of course, she took on Shaykh al-Ghalayini. For two hundred pages, she dissected his critique of her book, citing specific passages with page references, responding in detail and even correcting his Arabic (*The Girl and the Shaykhs*, pp. 353–356). She pointed out instances when he agreed with her, as when he claimed that Islam allows women to show their faces and their hands, yet he faulted "Miss Nazira" because she had claimed that women could reveal their necks and arms (al-Ghalayini 1929, p. 44).

"How could you say that I corrupted al-Baydawi's language? It is not I who corrupt; it is you. Look at page 121 where you corrupt what I wrote on page 233."

She scoffed at his preposterous statement that nine misguided people had written the book and that a mere girl, a "graduate of secular and convent schools, is unable to write such a work, to encompass the Sunna and to comprehend the verses." To this aspersion she retorted, "Don't deny me knowledge or claim I cannot write. Do not deny God the right to guide whom he wishes. He is the Almighty and he guided my study and education." In fact, she protested, it was precisely her Christian education that had confirmed her belief in Islam and her realization that Islam is more committed to women than any other religion (*The Girl and the Shaykhs*, pp. 16, 19, 132, 115). Addressing her readers directly, she begged them not to trust al-Ghalayini but to read her book and then judge for themselves.

Again, she pointed out the contradictions at the heart of his discourse: "What does the shaykh hope to gain from blackening the pages? And this after having acknowledged that men and women are intellectual equals and that neither is superior to the other. It is he who asserted that men and women have mutual rights and obligations and that renewal is the secret of life and that whatever is not renewed is destroyed and that we have to renew ourselves in accordance with our needs and we have to develop in accordance with our times" (*The Girl and the Shaykhs*, p. 259).

She accused him of taking revenge on her for having pointed out the contradictions and double standards in his 1908 book: "I hear that you screamed to the people that it was the Christian missionaries and those whom they had bought who had written and distorted it? No,

Shaykh al-Ghalayini, missionaries had nothing to do with this book. I wrote it without interruption day and night for months. I was in a room alone with nothing but pen, ink, notebooks, the Qur'an and the Sunna and the words of the imams. My only visitors were my father who from time to time checked in to see how the work was progressing and the Arabic tutor whenever I needed help on a point of grammar. There were no missionaries or non-missionaries, no men wearing turbans or hats or tarbushes, there were no atheists, no secularists, no teachers, and no lawyers with me" (*The Girl and the Shaykhs*, pp. 21–22, 309).

Of course, anyone without bias could see that *Unveiling and Veiling* was no work of missionaries. It lacked the central theme of the colonizing project: a denigration of the society as a whole. Feminist postcolonial theorists have analysed the European ploy to use the perceived oppression of women to gauge the moral and intellectual caliber of the society. Highly judgmental, such a position argues that there is something inherently wrong with a society in which men seem to be sanctioned to discriminate against their women. Colonizers argued that such societies had to be saved for universal civilization through the mediation of an outside, civilized agent, i.e. the colonizing missionary. Women became the key to social transformation. Colonial rhetoric turned men like this into barbarians and their women into victims, but ironically also the potential route to salvation. If they could be rescued, the nation as a whole might become part of world civilization. The fundamental gender justice of Islam, the relentless theme of Nazira's book, was hardly conducive to their arguments.

Nazira's point was different. She was not alleging that Arab, Lebanese, or Muslim men were uncivilized or that there was something wrong with their society. It was the shaykhs who were responsible for preventing the nation from improving through the elevation of women to full partnership with men (*Unveiling and Veiling*, pp. 52, 59, 85, 113). Taking her cue from the Qur'an but also from John Stuart Mill, she made the case for women's intellectual and spiritual equality with men and their right to participate in running the affairs of home and society. Like Mill, she advocated elite social responsibility by appealing to bourgeois women to lead the struggle for all women's rights.

Citing religious sources to show what a bad Muslim he was, she chided al-Ghalayini for slander and demanded that he bring proof of missionary involvement in *Unveiling and Veiling*. If he could not, then he must stop preaching lies! Was he dwelling on the matter of authorship because he was incapable of debating the content with her, or because he was too proud to debate openly with "the Girl," even when he knew that "God has forbidden pride"? Did he really think he could get away with all his contradictions?

"In this topsy-turvy condition the Shaykh has earned himself some names that have cast a veil over the eyes of the beholders, and those who have read *Unveiling and Veiling* will see that veil for what it is … so let him strut now because there will be no room for pride after time has judged him" (*The Girl and the Shaykhs*, pp. 13, 15, 20, 18, 36). There will be no room for pride because she would demonstrate how al-Ghalayini had willfully twisted her words.

"Is it possible that an Arab should forbid research into a social custom that was widespread among the nation's people and to which a group of Muslims and non-Muslims adhered? Is there not a Tradition that calls those who see the truth and do not speak about it the 'mute devil'? Clearly, the Iranian al-Afghani was right when he once said that things had deteriorated to such an extent that it was as though non-Muslims knew what is in the Qur'an and Muslims did not" (*The Girl and the Shaykhs*, pp. 75–76).

She answered Shaykh al-Ghalayini's accusations with long passages taken from *Unveiling and Veiling*, quoting herself for over thirty pages (*The Girl and the Shaykhs*, pp. 264–300). Each passage addressed to al-Ghalayini as a riposte to some accusation he had made in *Views* was introduced with something like: "And am I not 'the Girl' who said …", and the passage might end with: "How have you, dear Shaykh, made it lawful for your pen to write that the aim of my book is the destruction of Islam as though Islam were not my religion?" Alternatively she might write: "Are these the kinds of statements from my book that you have used, O Shaykh, to claim that my aim was to strike a blow at my religion, the religion of Islam?" [see for example, *The Girl and the Shaykhs*, p. 268].

How could he accuse her of wanting "to destroy the veil with a sword or cannon"? She wanted women to understand their rights and duties in Islam and to decide for themselves if they wanted to cover their faces or not. No, she did not want to turn women against men. No, she had not called past shaykhs ignorant, and she cited passages from her book in praise of some, pointing out that it was al-Ghalayini who had denigrated these predecessors (*The Girl and the Shaykhs*, pp. 314, 325, 296–302).

She complained that *Views* had wasted her time because she had been compelled to sort the roses from the thorns of his vicious criticism! She even had to correct his Arabic. How ridiculous was his claim that the collapse of the Roman Empire was due to the fact that women were not veiled and they mixed with men. The good Shaykh should read Montesquieu to learn the real reasons for the decline and fall of the Roman Empire. She declared sarcastically: "The power you attribute to the veil has been woven on a loom of weak brains; it is a fantasy you are weaving." As for his accusation that her writing was dangerous because it was full of "magical seductiveness," she retorted that there was nothing wrong with writing well, or in using the rhymed prose that was popular at the time, or in composing poems (*The Girl and the Shaykhs*, pp. 256, 252–253, 54–55, 95).

Having revealed his deceit and questionable scholarship, she warned: "Fear God! Fear God, O Shaykh! Islam is my religion." Note how obvious it was to her that she was a Muslim and, therefore, that her Druze religion of birth was not in contradiction with her affiliation and utter commitment to the orthodox Muslim community.

Not only did she consider herself to be fully Muslim but she also compared her situation with that of Aisha, the favorite wife of Muhammad and Mother of the Faithful, when the people slandered her: "Have you made slander lawful for yourself? How could you say that I diminished and besmirched women in my book? ... Is this how you debate with a woman who is in conformity with the will of the Almighty?" (*The Girl and the Shaykhs*, pp. 272, 274).

Nazira was referring to an incident in the life of the first Muslim community. During one of Muhammad's military campaigns, his wife Aisha had been left behind in the desert after the Prophet had called for camp to be struck. Her howdah-bearers had not noticed she was not in the camel litter because she was light and men could not look inside the private quarters of one of the Prophet's wives to check if she was there. A young man found Aisha alone and lost in the desert and he had led her home. Rumor had it that Aisha and the young man were lovers. Then the following verse was revealed to Muhammad: "And those who accuse free women then do not bring four witnesses, flog them eighty times and do not admit any evidence from them ever; and these it is that are the transgressors" (Qur'an 24: 4). Muhammad understood the connection between this verse about false accusation and the scandal surrounding the couple walking out of the desert, and he protested against the Muslims' censure of his innocent spouse. Aisha was exculpated and the slanderers condemned: "Surely those who love that scandal should circulate respecting those who believe, they shall have a grievous chastisement in this world and the hereafter" (Qur'an 24:19). Nazira felt herself to be comparably reviled.

In this second book, Nazira was addressing another set of readers. Whereas in the first the abundant citations from religious texts come without references, in the second a scholarly apparatus is included. The first book was for religious scholars who did not need volume and page references since they had memorized much of the material. The second book addressed readers less marinated in these religious texts and who might not have been able to follow the argumentation of the first. Was she trying to empower women against those shaykhs who did not have their mothers', sisters', and daughters' interests at heart?

The year 1929 would have seemed to be auspicious for the appearance of a book like this. It was the year of the first Arab women's conference, a time when individual and national women's actions came together for the first and not the last time. Why did her strategy not succeed? What went wrong?

7

WHAT WENT WRONG?

Why was Nazira Zeineddine excluded from the galaxy of modern Islamic reformists? This chapter bridges the two halves of her split life: her empowered youth and her silenced adulthood.

"The Girl" was the first woman to write an entire book that argued for women's rights in Islam and their unconditional intellectual equality with men. Warning against immorality, she had explicitly not called for complete unveiling, only for women to keep their faces open to the sun. She knew her sources well and had checked with reputable authorities before publishing anything, so she was not prepared for the vehemence and venom of the shaykhs' responses. But she should have anticipated some reaction to the tone of the book and the gender of its author.

Merciless in her exposure of the shaykhs and their flagrant misreading of the Qur'an and Sunna, she highlighted their contradictory statements and their anxiety about women in a tone dripping with sarcasm: "O, Gentlemen Opponents, are you afraid of losing control over your women should they be educated?"

The reader of *The Girl and the Shaykhs* can feel Nazira trembling with rage and frustration that she deflects by sometimes referring to herself in the third person as the "Muslim Girl." At other times, she addresses herself in the second person. Fearless, she mocks al-Ghalayini: "Poor Shaykh, he couldn't restrain his angry soul from vengeance. He could find nothing in your book except what accorded with religion and reason and the welfare of the Muslims so he made things up."

Again and again, she cites parts of her work that the shaykhs misquoted or incorrectly interpreted. Unlike the earlier wealth of quotations from the Qur'an and Traditions without scholarly apparatus, the second book includes scholars' and shaykhs' reactions to her book with specific references. Where Qasim Amin had responded to the debacle surrounding his 1899 *Liberation of Woman* with another book, *The New Woman,* that does not name any of his detractors, Nazira lashes out at individuals. She is fierce in her sarcasm, turning the shaykhs' own accusations against them: "Gentlemen and Shaykhly Opponents, you should read more before you write your books and letters in which you oppose the Girl's behavior so that you would know what our Master Ali, the Leader of the Faithful, said and do not have to rely on the missionaries." She relished the opportunity to cite missionary influence on the shaykhs who were not sufficiently learned to be able to find proof texts on their own.

For pages she listed books and scholars these carping shaykhs should have consulted before attacking her. For example, Shaykh Said al-Jabi had happily cited Traditions about women lacking in religion and intellect without checking whether they were sound or not. And even if they could find Traditions about women's inferiority in Bukhari should they automatically believe them? Could it be that all Traditions that are positive about women are weak and all that are negative are sound? Who can guarantee that al-Bukhari was not compelled by his circumstances and influenced by those who did not think well of women?

To find the answers to such questions all they had to do was to open pages 5, 8, and 11 of *Usul al-kafi* by Muhammad b. Yaqub al-Baraqi who died in AH 274. He should read *Kitab al-majalis* of Muhammad b. 'Ali Babawayh al-Qummi, who died in AH 381, and page 66 in *Kitab al-wasa'il* by Muhammad b. Hasan al-Hurr al-'Amili. Shaykh Salah al-Din should read page 229 from the 1885 *Kitab nahj al-balagha,* where he could read the story about 'Ali, the Prophet's cousin and son-in-law, who told Salim ibn Qays al-Hilali that people make up interpretations to suit their interests and that Muhammad had condemned such deceitfulness (*The Girl and the Shaykhs*, pp. 40–43).

It is her opponents who have relied on the missionaries, not she. It is they who are deficient in religion and reason, not she. She also singles out specific institutions for special censure. Students of the venerable institutions of the Egyptian Azhar, the Iraqi Najaf, and the Indian Deoband are misguided: "You should not say what you say. These statements of yours allow people to derive meanings that harm the reputation of Islam." She adds provocatively that while Oxford University produces graduates who are world leaders, these Islamic institutions, despite their numerous students and much longer courses of study, have produced none.

She calls her detractors "racket rousers." They raise a ruckus as long as others are shouting, "We don't want! We don't want!" When the din dies down they shut up because they have nothing to say. They simply parrot the cries and opinions of others.

When she asks the Opponents what they thought unveiling meant and they replied indecent exposure, she chastises them for deliberately twisting her words. Quoting a Tradition, she says, "Whoever practices deceit with a Muslim is not a Muslim." In other words, those who opposed her were not Muslims because they knew that when she used the word unveiling she meant nothing more than uncovering the face. As Abu Hanifa once said, "Women's faces are not 'aura, shameful, and those words are inscribed in letters of light on the Tablet of Truth." Her Opponents clearly had not read page 232 of *Unveiling and Veiling* where she had given a clear definition of unveiling and had expressed her utter distaste for any kind of indecent exposure. She caught them in a familiar tactic: quoting piecemeal and out of context (*The Girl and the Shaykhs*, pp. 45–50).

A prominent opponent was Shaykh Salim Hamdan. She disparaged his *Civilization and the Veil* for being barren of ideas; its Arabic was so abysmal it had to be corrected. She could do no more than to ask God to forgive him. His only proof that the veil is Islamic came from belief, not knowledge, that it is the badge of Islam. Didn't he know that women of other religions are veiled (*The Girl and the Shaykhs*, pp. 251–263)? He returned the favor a little later, ridiculing *The Girl and the Shaykhs* as little more than repetition of *Unveiling and*

Veiling and a collection of fulsome praise that did not add anything to the overall content of the book: "Who cares to read these passages heavy with praise especially when they know who you are and what you know?" (Bu Matar, 2008, p. 31).

Shaykh Yusuf al-Faqih, her father's colleague who had earlier approved the manuscript, also criticized her for publishing so much praise of the first book in the second. No shrinking violet, Nazira denounced him in "The Girl and the Shaykhs on Unveiling and Veiling," an article she published in *Al-Ahd al-Jadid* on 27 January 1930 (Bu Matar, 2008, pp. 39, 126). Describing a meeting with what she calls "enlightened Muslim women," she cites an unnamed "brilliant" woman who is given four pages to produce verbatim quotations of her book. Brilliant women, in other words, recognize and understand her brilliance.

The defenders of unveiling, she insisted, were merely calling for women's right to expose their faces to the sun. However, if the verse about modesty and averting the eyes from the opposite sex is their sole proof, then they should remember that the same injunction was directed at men and, therefore, they, too, should cover their faces. Could it be that they had not remembered that the verse is addressed to men and women? And if men refuse to cover their faces and still want to impose the veil on women, "then I beg you to acknowledge that the justice and respect for religion that you profess are but a trick to allow you to oppress your mother, your sister, your wife and to be unjust to them." Heedless of the danger of attacking shaykhs, let alone humiliating them, she decries their ignorance and duplicity. Citing several Traditions concerning unveiled Muslim women around Muhammad, she asked: "Gentlemen, have you read in the Book or any Tradition a command against unveiling? Surely not! Have you found one concerning covering the face? Surely not! Why do you disobey God's command and that of the Prophet? When a man covers the face of a woman, Gentlemen, he is committing a certain injustice" (*The Girl and the Shaykhs*, pp. 182–189).

For some, her tone was offensive, for others, brave. Here was a woman who used men's polemical language that was considered part of accepted, orthodox parlance among religious authorities only.

Since the middle of the nineteenth century, liberal and modernist Muslims had been demanding reform in the teaching and practice of Islam. They had called for freedom to engage in *ijtihad* (independent interpretation), since God endowed all humans with reason. Analysing the writings of liberal thinkers who contested the shaykhs' monopoly on interpretation of Islamic sources, sociologist Charles Kurzman presents debates about "who may speak" and who may therefore practice *ijtihad*. Many reformists rejected the need for orthodox credentials, and "expressed confidence in their own qualifications – seminary training, modern education, or personal virtuosity – as compared both with their scholarly opponents and the 'masses'. [Some even defended] education in secular subjects [to] prepare students properly for the practice and study of Islam." They viewed modernity in a guardedly positive light, praising innovations Europeans had introduced, even while criticizing their betrayal of these ideals and values. The "distinctiveness of the modernists lay in seeing modernity as a promising avenue for cultural revival [even if they] disagreed vehemently among themselves as to the extent to which cultural revival must erase existing cultural forms" (Kurzman, 1998, pp. 23–25; 2002, pp. 11–17).

Debate, often intense and hard-hitting, was the norm in Islamic discourse. Anthropologist Talal Asad has written that wherever Muslims have "the power to regulate, uphold, require, or adjust correct practices, and to condemn, exclude, undermine, or replace incorrect ones, there is the domain of orthodoxy ... Argument and conflict over the form and significance of practices are therefore a natural part of any Islamic tradition" (Asad, 1986, p. 16). In the late 1920s, emotional affirmation of correct belief and practice informed the repertoire of Islamic discourse. Yet until Nazira joined the fray women had rarely been acknowledged as participants.

Having read the classics and the modernists, she not only knew but also used their style of argumentation, even if at times she did come across as gratuitously provocative. To say once: "How dare you,

Shaykh!" and to ridicule another's language might have worked in a text that was otherwise more sober. But how many times could she repeat "Be fair, Shaykhs!" without losing her readers? Carried away by her own rhetoric, she poses six strident questions in response to an accusation. Each question is preceded by "And is there in what I have written" and it is followed by the charge. For example, "And is there in what I have written a demand that the state should oppose the freedom of veiled women? God is witness to the oppression that Shaykh al-Ghalayini has committed against me. The Prophet (peace be upon him) said, 'If a mountain oppresses a mountain, the oppressor will be leveled'" (*The Girl and the Shaykhs*, p. 308). The repeated outrage obscured the urgency of her message.

The sarcasm and ridicule sometimes slide into insult, especially in her colorful invectives directed against al-Ghalayini: "No sooner have you written a page or a phrase, than you forget what you have just said and you contradict it. By the time you have written the third page you have forgotten what you wrote in the preceding pages and you again contradict yourself. The reader of your *Views* sees his mind about to drown in your piled-up phrases that a wild storm has whipped into lashing waves. He can find no escape to the shores of truth" (*The Girl and the Shaykhs*, p. 340).

But it was not only his digressions and contradictions that she deplored; she also contested his misleading claims about what she had written. She went through his lists of her so-called mistakes and corrected his deliberate twisting of her words. For example, citing page 125 of *Views,* she reproached him for consciously misinterpreting her use of the word *juyub* or bosom that must be covered that is found in Qur'an 24:31. He was intervening in a critique she had directed at the fourteenth-century exegete Abdullah bin Ahmad bin Mahmud al-Nasfi. He claimed that on page 218 she had inaccurately interpreted the word to mean an opening or split in clothes and not the bosom. Where, she demanded to know, did he find that interpretation?

"Where in my book did you find the word 'split,' or even something resembling it so that you could claim what you claimed? Had you read my book with a heart empty of desire and intent to find fault you would have understood my contestation of al-Nasfi's argument" (*The Girl and the Shaykhs*, p. 368). Nowhere in her text did she allow for *juyub* to mean anything other than the bosom that must be covered.

While Nazira was right to point out mistakes, both factual and rhetorical, she had not known how great a role her gender and ultimately her religious affiliation would play in the reception of her writings. Further, unaware of the gold standard of evidence to which she would be held accountable, she opened herself up to censure with some casual generalizations and arbitrary numbers. Comparing the "veiled and unveiled worlds," she asked "how can we imagine that one and a half billion are wrong and we are right?" She had read in newspapers, she writes without specification, that "thousands of Muslim women in Samarqand and Tashkent in the Far East rebelled against the *burqa*', calling it a form of tyranny. Fifteen thousand women in Samarqand markets walked through the streets unveiled. In Tashkent, women walked in front of twenty-five thousand men to the public square where they burned their *burqa*'s: That is how they entered life and light" (*Unveiling and Veiling*, pp. 111, 122). It was her blanket dismissal of men who forbid the permitted and permit the forbidden that had enraged al-Ghalayini with his neat mustache.

In the first heady days after the appearance of *Unveiling and Veiling*, she welcomed the accusation that it was impossible for "the Girl" to have written such a book. After all, the nineteenth-century Syrian poet, Warda al-Yaziji, had also been accused of not writing her poems. However, when the death of each of the supposed ghostwriters did not stop the flow of her ink, detractors had to acknowledge her authorship. In her 1924 elegy for Warda al-Yaziji, four years before Nazira published *Unveiling and Veiling*, Mayy Ziyada wrote: "Do not believe the accusation directed against her, and other women, that men write for her. The greatest proof is that in the beginning they claimed that her father and brothers, Habib and Khalil, had composed it for her. Then they died and she eulogized them. So the people said: 'Shaykh Ibrahim is alive. He must be the one who composed the eulogies in her name.' Then Shaykh Ibrahim died and she eulogized him in verses that are among the most profound and sincere of anything she had ever written"(Badran & cooke, 1990, p. 242).

Nazira did not take the authorship charge seriously and mocked al-Ghalayini's misrepresentations: "I never claimed I was more knowledgeable than ancient or contemporary scholars. I am not proud. I am merely a servant of my religion, my country, and my people and a defendant of my rights and the rights of my sisters. God gave me reason, light, and guidance and, unlike you, I do not want to neglect them" (*The Girl and the Shaykhs*, pp. 15, 17).

One of her defendants, Mademoiselle Kandiyani, was the editor of the leading French paper *Le Figaro*. She scorned the opponents who could not believe that Miss Zeineddine had written this book because she was so young. That in itself was proof of her authorship: only someone so young could have written such a book! Responding to those who thought her too young to be erudite, Nazira adopted the tone of a schoolmarm when discussing the Traditions she had cited and that they had claimed were weak. She contemptuously pointed out that their claims contradicted the Qur'an.

"Dear Shaykh, you did not use your mind ... the learned teacher should have liberated his mind as he was commanded to do ... Gentlemen Opponents, you should not say what you are saying because people will derive meanings harmful to the reputation of Islam" (*The Girl and the Shaykhs*, pp. 16, 44–45).

Youth may have helped her to say what others dared not say, but it also blinded her to the impact of her defiant and insolent speech. While Egyptian and Syrian feminists in the nineteenth and early twentieth centuries had been circumspect in acknowledging indebtedness to European / colonial influences, Nazira was not. She frequently referred to unveiled Western women who are respected and allowed to play important roles in their society. Drawing on her experience at the convent schools, she wrote about nuns who do not cover their faces. If they are not lacking in reason and religion, then why are Muslim women singled out? (*Unveiling and Veiling*, pp. 134,

138) These religious, unveiled Christian women from the West to whom Muslim parents entrusted their children, were respected, the schools in which they taught were clearly the best, so they should be emulated.

> The best way to build the best schools for Arabs and Muslims is to copy the best foreign schools and universities like Oxford, the Sorbonne, Columbia, Princeton and Harvard where minds are freed to soar into the open sky enlightened by new knowledge and attentive to the illuminating forces God gave them, purified of the germs of diseases or worn-out customs that are a disaster for the East. The West rose with the rise of its unveiled women. They did not pose men a threat. May men and women in the East awake! The sun of freedom has spread its rays over the East that should voluntarily and quickly follow the rightly guided path of the West.
>
> (*The Girl and the Shaykhs*, pp. 40, 60–62)

In a blatant provocation to Shaykh al-Ghalayini, she praised the missionaries: "these foreigners with their mission to the Arab world were saying what Muslims were saying, the only difference was that they were concerned with Christianity and we with Islam. The dispassionate among us will acknowledge that both religions agree in spirit and essence even if non-essential differences arise. How could it be otherwise when both have books God revealed from the Mother Book? Is not Jesus the Spirit of God and Muhammad His Beloved? Those who worship God, including missionaries, are brothers to us. They preach from the Old and New Testaments as the Muslims preach from the revealed Qur'an" (*The Girl and the Shaykhs*, pp. 27–28).

She knew that religious authorities and others would deplore Christian approval of her book, yet she quoted at length from Christians who sang her praises. She quoted Rashid al-Khuri, a highly respected intellectual known as "the Village Poet," who wrote in Brazil's Sao Paolo paper, *Fata Lubnan* #4197, that even if Nazira were to write nothing else this book alone would provide an echo of her generation. Commending the elegance of her writing he declared that not only Muslim women and men but also people of other

religions should read her. As a Christian, he found her characteriza-
tion of Islam so attractive he was tempted to convert. Nazira was not
afraid that quoting praise from a Christian might harm her case (*The
Girl and the Shaykhs*, pp. 29–34). Several priests published positive
articles, and Christian intellectuals Amin al-Rihani and Khalil Bey
Mutran were lavish in their praise, even though al-Rihani also wrote
to her on 25 April 1928 objecting to her excessive quotations (*The
Girl and the Shaykhs*, pp. 171–172; Bu Matar, 2008, p. 66). Dismayed
that her reliance on the Qur'an and Sunna bothered several readers,
she retorted, "were the readers of *Unveiling and Veiling* to strip away
Qur'anic verses and Traditions they would find nothing more than
the scrapings in the bottom of a pot, or dust dropped out of a bundle
of clothes" (*The Girl and the Shaykhs*, p. 139).

In her anxiety to prove her textual credentials, she had followed
the advice of her father's associates and included many scriptural passages. In the process, she ended up using the language and sources
that the shaykhs knew well. By so doing, she opened herself to attack
in kind. For every Qur'anic verse she cited they could retort with
another. For every Tradition she invoked, without the chain of
authorities customarily prefacing a citation, they had three. She
might interrupt an argument with a series of such quotations that cut
her reader's train of thought and weakened her argument. Bu Matar
also points to the questionable logic she employed, for instead of asking whether her arguments were in synch with religion, she asked
whether Islam confirmed her statements (Bu Matar 2008, p. 187).
Historian Elizabeth Thompson writes that scholars like al-Ghalayini
"dismissed the book's broader social and political argument by focus-
ing upon narrow legal debates about whether or not Islamic scripture enjoined the veil ... After 1928, it would be more difficult for
lay Muslims, male or female, to write with authority on the issue.
Learned ulama had vehemently reclaimed veiling as a matter of
religious law, not of personal choice or civil law" (Thompson 2000,
pp. 135, 136).

More problematic than tone, gender, and reliance on the shaykhs'
language was her self-presentation as a transcendental authority.

Framing the book as a religious text, she called the preface "*Fatihat al-kitab*," or "The Opening of the Book." Comparison with the Qur'an is explicit since that is also the title of the first chapter of the Qur'an, sometimes simply called the Book. She creates an ambiguous connection between the Qur'an and her book, so convinced is she of the righteousness of her argument.

As the daughter of a judge deeply versed in Islamic texts, she claimed an authority that would allow her to arbitrate between what was Islamic and what was not, what was a matter of personal law and what was not. Contending that the veil was not Islamic, she turned the polemic about the veil into a civil matter. In so doing, she was able to appeal to the French who were barred from involvement in matters which were simply religious: "In my book I called on the mandate powers not to interfere in religious affairs or to pressure women's commitments in any way" (*The Girl and the Shaykhs*, p. 113). The shaykhs, on the other hand, could not appeal to the French for help in their fight to cover women, precisely because they were insisting on the religious nature of the veil. Veiling was a civil matter, and those who tried to force women to veil in the name of religion were bad Muslims because Muhammad preferred uncovered faces. Moreover, they were delinquent subjects under French law.

In response to al-Ghalayini's demand for evidence that the shaykhs had pressured the government to impose mandatory veiling, she cited a letter from 'Abd al-Rahman al-Huss to Ahmad Nami Bey, president of Syria, listing ten shaykhs and civic leader signatories who thanked the president for forbidding women from leaving their homes unveiled (*The Girl and the Shaykhs*, p. 310). This was the same president who had written to Nazira on 7 April 1928, calling her noble and gifted, "the highest model of service to your nation that will be proud of you and people like you" (*The Girl and the Shaykhs*, p. 142). Here was another hypocrite.

On 2 October 1929, she once again wrote to Ponsot, summarizing the main arguments of *The Girl and the Shaykhs,* a book he could not read because he did not know Arabic (Bu Matar, 2008, p. 38). The French, in effect, became the third element between the religious authorities and the people. They were the good secularists whose power and commitment to neutrality in matters of religion in the colonies made them allies in the fight against the veil (*The Girl and the Shaykhs*, p. 170). In defense of her communication with the agent of French colonialism, she wrote, "I did not ask the mandate state, neither in my book nor in my letter to M. Ponsot, to free the Muslim woman because, as I wrote on page 14, the Muslim woman is free according to God's Book and the Sharia and the law and the highest principles of society. Islam guarantees her human rights" (*The Girl and the Shaykhs*, p. 64).

When she urged readers to look to the West where women were unveiled and the society enjoyed economic, social, and political prosperity, she did not anticipate the strong rejection that lay in store for her. Living in cosmopolitan Beirut where the French mixed with the Lebanese, she thought them worthy of comparison, especially since many of their women were established in professions and admired for their knowledge (Bu Matar, 2008, p. 69).

John Stuart Mill's fierce defense of women's equality and freedom in *The Subjection of Women* informed her position. When she urged opponents to bring proof that women cannot lead even though they knew that many women had been leaders in Islamic history, she was invoking Mill who had objected to the claim that "men have a right to command and women are under an obligation to obey ... they are bound to show positive evidence for the assertions, or submit to their rejection. [Experience teaches that] raising the social position of women ... (is) the surest test and most correct measure of the civilization of a people or an age" (Mill 1869, pp. 2, 12). Nazira lauded Mill's advocacy of companionate marriage. His beloved wife Harriet Taylor had died in 1859, the year he published *On Liberty* and ten years before *The Subjection of Women*. Nazira noted that he had dedicated *On Liberty* to the soul that inspired his best thoughts. She cited his dedication to

> my friend and wife whose passion for truth and justice was my greatest support and whose approval of my work was my most

cherished achievement. Her share in this book is no less than mine ...
If it were possible for my pen to express half of the noble thoughts and
lofty sentiments buried with her, scholars would gain greater benefit
than from anything I write from my own thought and feelings without
the counsel of her unique mind.

Nazira begged Muslim men to "give back to your wife her stolen
rights, the most basic of which is the acknowledgment of her fullness
of mind and religion." Wasn't Mill right that antipathy to women's
equality and freedom was based on fear (*Unveiling and Veiling*, p. 85)?

Nazira thought she could work within both the Christian and
Islamic systems, but she finally failed. Her demands for changed gender norms and values were deemed too Francophile and the embroil-
ment of the French in this very internal problem was to have grave
political consequences. Many felt disenfranchised in a state run by
foreigners and their allies among the elites. Attacks on her, on advo-
cates of unveiling, and on the bookstores that sold her book turned
violent.

Not only did the conservative shaykhs attack her writings, vigi-
lantes also policed public spaces. They took it upon themselves to
intimidate women once again by throwing acid on those who ven-
tured unveiled into the streets, and to silence their voices by attacking their press. Some women wrote to Nazira saying they knew she
was trying to help them but the backlash was overwhelming, "all we
got was bitterness and more suffering and pain" (*The Girl and the
Shaykhs*, pp. 228, 312–313, 71). These developments were terrifying
and Nazira acknowledged her fear when she wrote, "I heard a voice
like that of my father saying to me: Daughter, break your pens and do
not write in defense of women's rights ... But this was merely a
dream" (*The Girl and the Shaykhs*, p. 68). This invocation of the father
who had pushed her to be outspoken was like a justification to with-
draw from public life and the blinding limelight in which she had
found herself. Although she did publish several articles in the 1930s
she did finally break her pens and disappear into the oblivion of
domestic life.

PART II

8

MARRIAGE

Nazira lived with her parents until she was thirty years old, alternating between the Karakol Druze house in Beirut and summers in Ayn Qani. There they continued to share the mansion with the imperious Amira, Said Bey's sister-in-law. Samia Saab recalled that Grandmother Amira "wanted her brother-in-law to be attentive to his family. She overwhelmed Hala, Nazira, and Munira. During the 1930s she was reading the London *Times* daily, and she knew the biographies of many famous women, especially in America and England. Our brother Raja used to call her Queen Victoria. Said Bey pushed Nazira to write, and supported her at a time when the entire society was opposed to change. After his return from Istanbul he was greatly respected, especially by my grandmother. Said Bey was called *qadi al-qudat* or judge of judges."

In the first years after the books scandal, Nazira and her father continued to write and act in ways not calculated to please the shaykhs. In December 1930, Said Bey officiated at a "modern wedding" held at the Ayn Qani house and Nazira was one of the witnesses. Applying Islamic and civil law together, Said Bey explicitly consulted the bride concerning the marriage contract. Although Islamic law calls for a bride's consent, in practice the men in the family tended to finesse that stipulation.

Everything the Zeineddines did was now open to conservative scrutiny and some shaykhs had found a loophole and took him to court. In the summer of 1932 they lost, not having reckoned with the power of this much loved lawyer who refused to tolerate their attack on the personal freedom of the modernizers (*Al-Safa'* #1352, 2 June 1932; Bu Matar, 2008, pp. 212–213). Failure to prosecute one of the leaders of the reformist movement did not stop the conservatives and the gap between the opposing sides yawned ever wider.

Said Bey sent his sons Munir and Kamil to the military Madrasat al-Hikma, and they became officers in the Lebanese army. Some undisclosed problems that Munir had with French officers led to life imprisonment. Said Bey was so outraged that a son of his should offend the French that he disinherited him. During the late 1930s, Munir was given the choice between staying in prison and going into exile in Sidi Bil'abbas in Algeria to fight for the French Legion Étrangère (Foreign Legion). He preferred the latter option, left Lebanon, and never again saw his family.

The 1930s were the years of women's struggles for suffrage in many Muslim countries, and after 1934 the issue became acute when Turkish women were given the right to vote and to be elected. This also was the decade in which Lebanese politics took a turn that institutionalized Druze disempowerment. In 1932, the French conducted what was to be the last popular census in twentieth-century Lebanese history. The census emphasized religious identification as the basis for the proportional allocation of political positions in a system that came to be called confessionalism. The contested results of the census put the Maronites as the most numerous community, with Sunnis and Shiites following, the Druze a distant fourth and the thirteen other religious communities trailing behind. Thus it was that the position of president was given to the Maronites, prime minister to the Sunnis and speaker of parliament to the Shiites. The Druzes, who had wielded great power in the past and whose religious intelligentsia had been considered on a par with the Sunnis, were marginalized. Kamal Jumblat (1917–1977), the leader of the Lebanese Druze community from the 1950s, wrote that it was the census and its repercussions that gave the Maronites, in the past primarily peasants and merchants, a political power they had never before enjoyed. The French Mandate "put total power into their hands. It was a free gift that they did not deserve" (Joumblatt, 1978, p. 96). The bitterness is palpable. The Druzes finally had to deal with the fact that they had become a minority with no real influence in the new Lebanon the French were creating.

Yet with the assurance of someone who felt protected by her status as an educated woman introduced into the local and French elite, Nazira continued to lecture and write for three years about women's lack of freedom. She published "Two Ills in Arab Society" in the February 1932 issue of *Al-Islah* and in April, "Oh East," a poem read to the Palestinian Club in Beirut, appeared in the magazine *Al-Farfur*. Most surprising was "An Open Letter to Mr. al-Ghalayini," published in *Al-Nida'* on 25 June 1932. Praising her opponent for his Islamic College talk about women's education, she proposed holding a session in his honor and awarding him the Lebanese and Syrian medals of Merit. Was she being sincere, or was this Nazira at her most cutting and sarcastic?

In October *Al-Farfur* published two answers to letters written by Ihsan Haqqi Bey, an Arabic teacher in Aligarh, India, in which he praised her for her defense of women's freedom. She thanked him, but she also took advantage of this opportunity to lament the ignorance and fanaticism of the Islamic *umma*. On 16 November, *Al-Nida'* published her eulogy for Iqbal 'Aliya given during the mourning ceremony held by the Association for Women's Awakening at the Lycée Français Laique.

In 1933, Nazira became a founding member and secretary of the Arab Women Workers' Union under the leadership of Nazik al-'Abid Bayhum. She threw herself into the life of the Union, and traveled around the country, addressing gatherings and reporting on these meetings in *Al-Ahrar* and *Al-Islah* of Buenos Aires. In March *Al-Rasid* published her address to the doctors' union about women who guide the first steps of every individual. Reiterating arguments from *Unveiling and Veiling* in all of these publications, she declared that no community could advance while its women were veiled and kept from honest work, and she called for Arab unity around the world, reform of Personal Status codes and educational curricula, and the separation of state and church.

In 1934 she gave only one talk and this in French. On 27 May at the opening session of the Arab Feminist Union conference, she talked about the progress Arab women were making in education and in the workplace (Bu Matar, 2008, pp. 40–41). However, protests and further signs of disapproval stopped even this meager flow of ink.

Nazira and her family started to contemplate the idea of marriage. After the publication of *Unveiling and Veiling* several suitors had presented themselves, one had even proposed to her directly in a letter, but Nazira had turned them all down. She was determined to hold on to the freedom she must have guessed she would lose once she married.

In fall 1937 the socialite Marquise Alice Shiha de Freij (1887–1964) held a dinner party to which she invited the Zeineddines and the al-Halabis of Baaqline. The Marquise was famous for her literary salon that regularly assembled Beirut's intellectuals and her dinner parties were legendary. Several days beforehand, her daughter Alexandra, who later became president of the Lebanese Red Cross where Nazira volunteered, called on her friend.

"Nazira, what are you going to wear on Saturday?"

"I don't know. Why do you ask?"

"Maman's invited Shafiq al-Halabi ..."

"You mean 'Don Juan of Beirut.' Are you up to your old tricks?" Nazira winked at her friend who was acquiring a reputation for matchmaking.

"You'll like him. He's charming, brilliant and rich."

"And he's fifteen years older than me. What's more, he's wallowing in the life of an eligible bachelor and he probably won't give me a second look."

"Yes, he will, if I have anything to do with it."

"I've heard Naayim al-Halabi's a witch and as for his sister Fedwa ..."

"Don't be silly! But I'm glad to hear that my plot's not too far out of line. Already thinking of the in-laws?"

Nazira blushed.

"Anyway you wouldn't be marrying them …"

"Is Asmahan coming?"

"Of course!" Alexandra was thrilled that the Arab world's diva would be in attendance. Six years later, Asmahan al-Atrash died in a car crash.

Meanwhile Shafiq was also coming under pressure. For years, his mother had been on the lookout for a bride but he had refused each one she proposed. By the late 1930s, however, it looked as though his political career was taking off, and he became more open to the idea of marriage. During one of the regular visits the al-Halabis paid to the Jumblats in neighboring Mukhtara, the powerful Nazira Jumblat (1889–1951) took Shafiq outside on to the huge veranda overlooking the valley and surrounding villages.

"Why don't you look over there?" she asked, nodding in the direction of Ayn Qani. Clearly she thought this was a good match, and it would be hard to say No to the Lady of the Mountain, as Nazira Jumblat was called. After the assassination of her husband Fuad in 1922, she had ruled over the Chouf from Mukhtara, widely extolled for her political acumen as she maneuvered between the French, the British, and the Druzes.

The de Freij dinner was a magnificent event. Smoked salmon, pate de foie gras, goose, lamb from New Zealand, and profiteroles and English trifle for dessert. Who would have thought that the world was still in the grip of the great depression and on the verge of another world war? Nazira looked enchanting in her peach princess gown and Shafiq was enchanted.

A few weeks later, the engagement was announced, and within a year Nazira married Shafiq al-Halabi (1892–1978), the forty-six-year-old president of the court of cassation. Son of Amin al-Halabi, the first doctor and surgeon to graduate from the American University in Beirut in 1882, Shafiq was the first Lebanese to earn a law degree from the Sorbonne in 1912. While he was in Paris he shared an apartment with Bishara al-Khuri, who decades later would become the first president of independent Lebanon. They were both law students but destined to follow very different paths in life.

Whereas Bishara chose to go to Cairo after graduation, Shafiq returned home shortly before the outbreak of World War I. Opposed to Ottoman rule, like Nazira's uncle Muhammad, Shafiq earned the ire of Jamal Pasha, the Slaughterer. Rumor had it that by 1915 he was on the list of those to be hanged. His father Amin knew that this was a dangerous moment and putting his son on a mule he sent him off into safe hiding somewhere in the Chouf for the duration of the war.

On his return to the family at the end of World War I, Shafiq became part of the French Mandate Administration in the newly declared Great Lebanon. When he was twenty-six, he worked in the same criminal court of appeals over which Said Bey presided. In 1920 he was appointed justice of the peace and director general of justice for the Alawites. The following year and for three years he was appointed officer of public education, equivalent to minister of education, a post that garnered him the French and Lebanese Légion d'honneur medals.

Shafiq's life, like most of his friends, revolved around politics. Many were to rise to the highest positions in government before and after independence in 1943. In 1924, at age thirty-two, he became a member of parliament and for almost twenty years he served on the French dispute settlement council. Between 1934 and 1939, he was president of the court of appeals and cassation (Bu Matar, 2008, pp. 19–22).

The most controversial period of his life began in 1936 when his friend Emil Edde, then president of Lebanon, founded the Constitutional (later called National) Bloc, a conservative pro-French Christian party. Edde appointed Shafiq its secretary, a position he retained under the next president, his good friend Alfred Naqqash (r. 1941–1943), until 1954. He was the only Druze member of the Bloc.

After the wedding, Nazira left Karakol Druze and moved to the apartment in Muhammad al-Hut street in Ras al-Naba' where Shafiq lived. Said Bey had given her a dowry of five hundred gold Ottoman liras, a fortune at the time. She looked all over Beirut and found a lovely villa in Sanayeh that she wanted to buy. Shafiq, however, refused. He preferred to use the money to buy fine furniture. They acquired lovely mirrors framed in mother of pearl, huge brass chandeliers, marquetry tables and Persian carpets. After all, he argued, as a politician who often invited people to his home, it was more important that the contents of the house were elegant than that they own their own place (or, perhaps, that she have a room of her own). This must have hit Nazira hard; it was the first sign that her earlier liberty was becoming a thing of the past. Summers from that time would be spent in the al-Halabi home in Baaqline with only brief visits to Ayn Qani.

On 25 September 1939, a short three weeks after the outbreak of World War II, the couple's eldest son Amin was born. In the beginning, the Lebanese feared that they were doomed to relive the horrors of World War I. Wadad Qurtas, who married a year after Nazira, recalls a city that ground to a halt as it submitted to a "wave of bitter pessimism, despair and confusion. Values and principles crumbled and people thought of their immediate concerns only without caring about what lay beyond" (Qurtas, 1982, pp. 139–143). But World War II largely passed Lebanon by. The preoccupation of the British and French with the global conflagration allowed the pace of anti-colonial struggles in the Arab world to accelerate.

In 1941, President Naqqash appointed Shafiq governor of Beirut and the surrounding district that extended from Iskenderoon in the north to Acre in the south. In July of that year Nabil was born. Two years later, shortly before Lebanese independence, Nazira gave birth to their last son, Arij.

On the occasion of each birth, a cedar was planted in the Baaqline garden, and acquaintances sent the parents poems of congratulations. When Nabil was born, his uncles' Arabic tutor Jamil Fakhuri sent a poem in which he waxed lyrical about Shafiq al-Halabi, the incomparable governor whom everyone loved, and Nazira who had contributed so much to the welfare of Muslim women (Bu Matar, 2008, p.13). In Arij's apartment hangs an anonymous paean to the parents; it celebrates his name, which means fragrance.

Nazira with Arij (courtesy of Said Zeineddine)

During World War II the hold of the French loosened and the family spent most of the war in the mountains, frequently visiting Ayn Qani. The larger family were divided in their loyalties to the French. Whereas the Zeineddines and the al-Halabis were supportive of the colonial presence, some of the cousins were not. In 1940 Nazira's

cousin Najla Saab was elected president of the Arab Feminist Union. In that capacity she led a major demonstration against the French in 1943. She was nine months pregnant and yet she was at the forefront of those demanding the liberty and independence of the country.

Over the years, the two cousins, who in 1915 had together recited Turkish poetry to Jamal Pasha and thus secured the release of Muhammad Zeineddine, had drifted apart. Whereas Nazira disappeared after the early 1930s, Najla became increasingly prominent. In 1944, she represented Lebanon at the Arab Women's Conference that Huda Shaarawi convened in Cairo. Two years later, she again represented Lebanese women at the UNESCO conference. She pursued her nationalist feminist activities until her death in 1971 and she was awarded several national medals (Nuwayhid, 1986, pp. 172–173).

Some time late in the war, she sent her daughter Samia and a group of about thirty Zeineddine children up to Ayn Qani to escape the bombing in Beirut. "She was sure," Samia recollected, "that we would be safer in the mountains with Jiddu in that wonderful house with its secret doors, tunnels, and storage rooms. The four-meter thick walls assured safety." Indeed, it was in such shelters that the current Jumblat residents passed much of the 1980s wars of the mountains.

"Upon our arrival at the house," Samia smiled at the memory, "who should we see on the terrace but Jiddu surrounded by French officers. 'Come here, kids! Let me introduce you to these nice officers!' We stayed only a few days downstairs in the lower salon where mattresses had been laid out on the floor and then we returned to Beirut."

Independence was not good for Shafiq al-Halabi. On assuming the presidency in 1943, his former roommate Bishara al-Khuri (r. 1943–1952) relieved Shafiq of his post as governor of Beirut. His gubernatorial tenure was bracketed by the birth of two sons. Because of their friendship, but probably also because he wanted to distance someone who had held a position of power under the former regime, Bishara al-Khuri offered Shafiq the embassy in Paris, an ideal post for one who owed so much of his power and prestige to the French.

Shafiq, however, refused. He hoped that the French were not gone for good and that the Bloc might regain power. It was a gamble and he lost.

Between 1943 and 1954 Shafiq was unemployed, and the family lived off their land, which stretched from Baaqline to Mukhtara. Shafiq started a process he pursued for the rest of his life: he sold vast tracts of land planted with olives, grapes, and figs that the al-Halabis had long owned. The basis of the al-Halabi wealth was their land and Shafiq's political ambitions were to cost them dearly. This was the last period Nazira spent time in Ayn Qani with her parents.

After the war, the al-Halabis returned to Ras al-Naba. Like their mother before them, the sons attended the Lycée Français Laïque close to their home. Her son Nabil recalled that "Maman loved having our friends over to play in the garden behind the apartment building. She would run after us, sandwich of labneh, tomatoes, or olives and olive oil in hand to make sure we had our afternoon snack. At other times, she would stand on the stairs waiting for each one to pass and hand him his sandwich as though it were a baton in a relay race. Our house was always full, with people asking Poppa for work and favors. Visitors were entertained in one of the two large salons with the fancy furniture. We gathered in the smaller parlor."

Arij recalled people seeking his father's help to resolve disputes, especially between Druzes and Christians. "He was friendly with everyone, but it was not a comfortable atmosphere for children, so we would escape the house as soon as possible to play with friends or to go hunting. I remember President Alfred Naqqash," his face lit up at the memory. "He played with me and let me ride on his back. Father was harsh. He didn't like to play or to tell jokes. He was very strict about lunch and dinner times. Lunch was at 12 sharp and dinner at 7. There was very little conversation at the dining table. He wasn't interested in us because we were so young. He did not do anything with us. He didn't help with our homework although Maman did. After dinner he would retire to his bedroom/study. And he closed the door."

Only once while the boys were growing up did they have any idea that their mother had written anything of importance. One of Nabil's high-school friends told him that some classes were studying her poetry. Presumably this was the anonymous poetry she had included in *Unveiling and Veiling* that no one had noticed at the time of its publication.

Nineteen forty-eight was the year of the war between the Palestinians and the Jews who fought to make the Balfour Declaration a reality. In May a newly established Israeli state was declared as the national home of the Jews; all Jews anywhere in the world had the "right to return" to the land they had left two millennia ago. Waves of Palestinians poured into Lebanon to escape the Nakba, or the Catastrophe, as they called the war. Refugee camps were set up in several districts, and although they were supposed to be temporary, most remain in place today. In July, Nazira's brother Kamil was decorated for the role he played in the Malkiya war against the Israeli forces.

While war was raging in the south, Shafiq campaigned in the Chouf for parliamentary elections. Again he sold land to defray the expense. Much to his disappointment and later anger, he lost. He then sought political office by other means.

In 1949, the Kurdish Husni al-Zaim successfully staged a bloodless coup in Syria, and he inspired opposition parties in Lebanon, among them members of the National Bloc. They all wanted to explore the possibility of a copycat coup in Beirut (Tarabulsi, 2008, pp. 194–195). Nabil remembers Emil Edde coming to the house one day when he was eight. He was hiding in a cupboard where his mother stored the chocolates. Afraid to be caught red-handed, he had stayed quiet as a mouse while the men deliberated.

"A few days later, Poppa left for Damascus."

The Husni regime, however, was short-lived; within a few months Adib Shishakli staged his own coup, threw al-Zaim into Mezze prison and executed him. With him died the hope for a Bloc revolution in Lebanon and these men had to come to terms with the new situation.

Although none of the family members still alive know how Said Bey reacted to his son-in-law's failure and fall from power, he must have been disappointed, to say the least. He left Beirut in 1951 to spend the last three years of his life in the mountains. By then he had become so fat – his grandsons attributed his obesity to his addiction to olives – that he had to have special furniture made for him, and by the end of his life he had difficulty walking. He had his own chair at the Jumblat palace of Mukhtara and a sedan chair in his home. One day shortly before leaving Beirut, he heard that the cavalcade of President Bishara al-Khuri was approaching. He called on his assistants to carry him down the stairs to greet the president. When al-Khuri noticed Said Bey, he stopped. Stepping out of his car, he humbly approached: "This," he told the people, "was my teacher." The president of Lebanon had interned as a legal clerk with Said Bey after graduating decades earlier from the Sorbonne with Shafiq al-Halabi.

After retiring from the court, Said Bey built a pool with a fountain and an orchard in Ayn Qani. When asked how he could afford this, he replied that his pension was not enough for him to be able to live in Beirut but that in Ayn Qani he could live off the land. Further murmurs of discontent in the family about the cost of the pool elicited this retort: "There are three things that attract the heart of a man: the tinkle of gold, the voice of a woman, the murmur of water. As for the tinkle of gold I have not heard it [indicating that he had always been poor], as for a woman's voice Hala has none and so what remains is the murmur of water. Do you want to deprive me of it?" In summarizing his life through these three precious things, Said Bey was recalling the Prophetic Tradition narrated by Ibn Hanbal: "I was made to love three things from your world: women, perfume, and the comfort of my eye is prayer."

When they were young, the boys spent a month each summer in Baaqline. Sensing that their parents were uncomfortable in the big house, with Grandmother Naayim al-Halabi and their maiden aunt Fedwa gossiping and criticizing, they preferred Jiddu's place. As soon as they appeared on the veranda Jiddu told Zaynab to bring the sugar-coated chickpeas. Then they played in his fabulous fountain-filled pool.

By 1951, Shafiq felt sufficiently confident of his political chances in the Chouf that he launched another campaign. Nabil remembers the summer day when the whole family set off on foot to visit the neighboring village of Ammatour. As always in his three-piece suit and city shoes, Poppa walked ahead with Maman and the boys following down the donkey path short-cut. The welcome was "fit for a prince." Plates piled high with homemade cookies were passed around and the boys had candies stuffed into their pockets to take home. The adults sat around the parlor sipping orange-blossom-laced lemonade and discussing the affairs of the village while the boys played outdoors. That family outing was particularly memorable because it was the only time they had all gone for such a long walk together. However, there were many other occasions when Shafiq visited the villages of the Druze Mountain to drum up support.

When he again failed in the 1951 elections, his disappointment was even greater than it had been three years before, and he never again sought an elected position. Moreover, he became adamant that his sons should not become involved in politics.

Meanwhile, Said Bey prepared for death. He had a cream-colored coffin made to fit his huge frame and he kept it under a bed so high that he had to climb up steps to reach it. Every six months or so, he would try it out for size, fearing that he might have outgrown it and the undertakers would not have time to make him another.

But Said Bey was not only concerned about death, he was also very concerned about life after death, keenly aware of his foibles, like the smoking and drinking that Druze shaykhs denounced (Hitti, 1928, p. 43). Samia Saab said that toward the end, "Jiddu started to worry about the hereafter and the road to it. It is very important for us that the Druze clerics invoke God's mercy upon us when we die. This invocation is made in series of three Allah *yarhamhu* (meaning may God have mercy on him), a remembrance ritual. Jiddu was afraid that the *mashayikh* who knew about his drinking arak and smoking would not participate in the invocation. So one evening just around sunset he invited them to the house. After offering them coffee, he told them of a dream he needed them to interpret.

"Hopefully all is well?" one of the shaykhs had exclaimed.

"I dreamt I died," Jiddu said, "and I went to heaven and I was afraid that I would not be admitted because I had smoked and drank arak and was not always polite. But I was told that I could go in because I had been honest and kind to people. What does this dream mean?"

In response to this hope for absolution before it was too late, they said: "Certainly you have been a wonderful judge ..."

Apparently they said nothing more, did not hint at the possibility of forgiveness. But when Said Bey died in 1954, the *mashayikh* did pronounce the invocation. Said Bey left all of his possessions to Kamil's as yet unborn son.

From exile, Munir wrote his mother to pay his condolences and to announce that he would see her in two years, having almost served his sentence. However, within a year he had died in a motorcycle accident somewhere in Indochina. No one told his mother, not even his younger brother Kamil, a brigadier by then, fearing she would not survive the news. Many remember Hala sending Munir gifts and gazing out of the window of her room in Ayn Qani waiting for the return of her lost son (Bu Matar, 2008, p. 15). A few months after Hala's death in 1959, a symbolic funeral was arranged for Munir with the *mashayikh* conducting all the rituals. There was no body, only a large photo. Behind the house is the tomb Said Bey built for the family. It contains the remains of Hala, their daughter Munira, their son Kamil, and the Turkish servant Zaynab.

In 1964, ten years after his demise, Said Bey finally acquired his heir. Kamil and his Belgian wife Monique Eugene had a child; he was to be their only offspring. Said was named for his grandfather. Long before Said was born, Kamil had been known as Abu Said, or Father of Said. That is the custom in many Arab countries: the father-to-be is called father of his father even if he is not married. Since Munir never married and no son of a daughter could perpetuate the Zeineddine name, it was left to the youngest son to continue the family line. With such a burden placed on his shoulders it is not surprising that he became interested in the family and particularly in his famous, albeit nearly forgotten, aunt. The hopes of the family, and especially Nazira, were invested in Said who was pampered by all.

Nazira with her nephew Said (courtesy of Said Zeineddine)

Photographs of his childhood show him surrounded by adoring adults. Once, when he was about six years old, he was sitting on Tante Nazira's lap in the Muhammad al-Hut apartment with his three uncles lined up in front of him. Whom did he love most? With the candor of children who have not yet understood how painful words can be he responded immediately "Arij." Nazira had laughed.

"When I was nine I stayed with Tante Nazira in Ras al-Naba. Father had been called up from the army reserve to serve during the 1973 war against Israel. Since my parents were divorced, I could not stay at home alone. I loved staying with my cousins and playing in the garden. She was constantly after me not to jump from the balcony lest I get hurt. She was so protective."

The decision to disinherit his children was based on Said Bey's belief that Nazira was secure with the al-Halabis, Munira with her teaching position in Maarif School would find her own way, and the misdemeanors of the black sheep of the family, Munir, had cost him his father's love. As for Kamil, the situation had become complicated. Although he had achieved moderate military success, since 1966 he had been a member of the Military Committee of the Arab League and until 1971 military attaché in Egypt, Iran, Turkey, Pakistan, and Iraq (Bu Matar, 2008, p. 17), he was a notorious spendthrift. The will provided for Kamil's *haqq al-intifa'*, or the right to benefit from the property. The *haqq al-raqaba*, the entire property, went to the expected heir who would take ten years to appear. By 1964, however, Kamil had spent most of the inheritance, and he had sold the famous fountain pool and orchards. When he died in 1991, his son Said inherited nothing beyond the crumbling mansion in Ayn Qani.

9

THE AFTERLIFE OF A WRITER

The second president of independent Lebanon was Camille
Chamoun (1952–1958). Aware of the National Bloc ambitions
and opposition to his predecessor, Chamoun wanted to appease
some of its leaders by offering them government positions.
However, when his representative came to the al-Halabi residence in
Ras al-Naba with the decree appointing Shafiq director of the administrative councils of electricity and transport, he disdainfully kicked
him out of the house.

It was then, and for the first time, that Nazira interfered in her
husband's political career. She was close to Chamoun's wife Zelfa and
had heard from her that the appointment was in the air. No sooner
had the door slammed behind the messenger than Nazira rushed into
the hallway. Tearfully, she begged Shafiq to reconsider the offer and to
think of the future of their boys who were watching this unprece-
dented scene in alarm. More practical than her intransigent husband,
she knew that without an earned income they would have to struggle
to make ends meet. He finally agreed.

He was once again the man to whom many turned for advice,
guidance, and help. In an era of remarkable prosperity but also widespread corruption, Shafiq al-Halabi remained scrupulously honest.
Like his father-in-law he opened the house to all who wished to see
him. A neighbor who went to school with the three al-Halabi boys
and who now lives in Kuwait remembers the couple fondly. "Aunt
Nazira and Uncle Shafiq were very popular and social. The house was
always full of people, and we were frequent visitors. Uncle Shafiq

was very intellectual; they both were. He would often recite long passages from Corneille. He loved Corneille, and I loved listening to him."

In an interview with Bu Matar conducted some time in the late 1980s, Amin credited his mother with giving "us boys what she had previously given to women and society, and in so doing she taught women close to her how to bring up their children. She did not rely on governesses although there were plenty available, because she wanted to be the only one responsible for our education. She treated people with the utmost respect and encouraged them to express themselves freely. Despite what people said, she believed there were limits to women's freedom that should not be transgressed. Although she encouraged my brothers and me to swim, and she took us to the St. Georges pool, she was utterly opposed to women swimming.

"Father's involvement in affairs of state led to Mother's withdrawal from the arena of debate, dispute, and social work, and she became preoccupied with our education. His insistence on honesty meant that he did not let his family use the governor's car (and Fawzi al-Halabi, the driver) because, as he used to say, it was the property of the state and not of the family … He did not let Mother return to her social work before she had perfected her domestic skills … in view of his sensitive political position he was annoyed that the tone of debate about women's liberation between his wife and the shaykhs had sharpened. Nevertheless her social work did not stop altogether. Every Wednesday she received visitors, who sought counsel about their problems" (Bu Matar, 2008, pp. 36, 21, 35). Amin's interview reflects the attitude of his two brothers with whom I spoke twenty years later. Her three sons were aware of her past engagement in women's issues and her subsequent disengagement. Although the period of Shafiq's political power did not last long it gave him the excuse to curb his wife's public activities. Political failure made him even more concerned to keep her out of the limelight. Moreover, the split between the Druzes and mainstream Muslim communities had become so institutionalized since independence that it would have been scandalous for a Druze woman to presume to tell Sunni and Shiite shaykhs how to interpret women-specific Islamic texts.

In 1958 civil war broke out and terror spread throughout the city. The US marines intervened and an uneasy calm returned. The sixties were the years of dolce vita in a Lebanon that had become the Switzerland of the Middle East, thanks to an influx of petrodollars. No longer merely a picturesque port town with streets lined with mulberry trees and fishermen whiling away summer days along its beachfront, Beirut had become the cultural hub of the region with more newspapers and publishing houses per capita than anywhere else in the Arab world. Arab intellectuals flocked to Beirut, and in the summer to the Baalbek festival to enjoy the vibrant international artistic scene. The al-Halabis, however, did not participate in these cultural and intellectual activities. Nazira worked behind the scenes in the Arab Academy and the Organization of the Syrian Union that later became the Arab Union. "La femme du jour" who had shone brighter than all the other suns at the Thabit palace forty years earlier was nowhere to be seen among the writers crowding Beirut's sidewalk cafes. She was absorbed in her sons' education.

In 1963, their middle son Nabil asked permission to study architecture in Rome. Nazira had never traveled, but she approved of his desire to attend the best architectural institution as long as he took his younger brother Arij with him. She was aware of the difficulties facing her sons because of their parents' political problems. She was still persona non grata in some circles and Shafiq had been humiliated with the crushing of his political ambitions. Although they did not intend to emigrate, the young men were to settle in Italy and thereafter only returned for short trips. Nabil spoke with amusement about how the years changed the way in which he and his brothers were sent off to their studies.

"We left by boat like all the students did in those days. The first time we left there must have been three hundred people to bid us farewell. Maman and Poppa and various members of the family were there. Just before boarding the ship, Poppa drew me aside and whispered: 'You're going to a foreign country. Make sure that you and your brother follow its customs. Don't meddle in politics and don't get sick!' Although he did not say it I knew he was warning me against venereal disease. Between 1963 and 1975, I returned to Lebanon every year for the summer and each time the number of people greeting and seeing me off dwindled. Finally, I took a taxi home!

"Maman would introduce me to aristocratic Druze women, ever hopeful I would marry into the community. She would write asking me to bring my best suit because there were going to be some cocktail parties." Ultimately, he married an Italian Catholic, thus ostracizing himself from the Druze community, that forbids marriage to non-Druzes.

In 1964, the year Said was born, Nazira and Shafiq sent their firstborn, Amin, to the London School of Economics, and they asked Nabil to accompany him. Shafiq had opposed all of Amin's choices for profession. He had not allowed him to enter into politics because of his own failures and disappointment with the state of Lebanese politics. When Amin wanted to go into law, his father's specialization, Shafiq again opposed him, probably for the same reasons. Business seemed less problematic and so it was that Amin was sent to the London School of Economics.

During that first trip to London, Nabil realized that all was not well with his older brother who was unduly upset by the slightest mishaps on the ship. After Amin had been in London for a while his communications with home stopped. ScotlandYard finally found him locked up in his room where for two weeks he had been writing all over the walls. The challenge then was how to get the disturbed young man back home. Surprisingly, help came from Ambassador Taqieddine, brother of one of Shafiq's former political rivals. A mark of the respect in which Shafiq was held, the ambassador accompanied Amin all the way back to Lebanon. After a run-in with an employer in an accountancy agency, he was fired and Amin never again worked. He stayed with his parents until their deaths.

The war of 1967 and the following student strikes in the capital scarcely touched this family that had bowed off the stage of Lebanese history. The growing violence in the region merely confirmed the parents' conviction that their two sons in Rome should stay where they were.

During the last fifteen years of his life Shafiq had no paid employment and yet not once did he or Nazira discuss their growing impoverishment with their sons. Nazira worked hard to ensure that all looked well to the world. More land had to be sold to cover the boys' tuition and board in Italy. Not only did he pay for this expensive foreign education, but Shafiq also refused to let his sons work during the summers when they returned home.

During the early 1970s Nabil recalls journalists visiting his mother. Public interest had turned from his father back to his mother after almost forty-five years of neglect. In June 1972 she spoke with Nadia al-Jurdi Nuwayhid who was assembling an encyclopedia of prominent Lebanese women. For Nuwayhid, Nazira's work completed Qasim Amin's project; her subtitle, *The Liberation of Women,* was more than homage to the Egyptian judge; it was an avowal of indebtedness, since there is much in *Unveiling and Veiling* that affirms Amin's positions. Both argued that the veil was not religious; it was not a sign of ignorance but its instrument that paralyses half of society. Both insisted that Islamic law calls for equality between men and women even if Nazira was more dogmatic about the need to give women absolute equality. For Amin it was enough that women be given primary education, Nazira demanded equal education to the highest levels, including also medical training.

Nuwayhid introduced Nazira as "one of those extraordinary people who come before their time and who point with certainty and courage to the wide horizons of the future." Nuwayhid asked her about the verbal and physical attacks to which she had been exposed: "Several times I was exposed to assassination attempts, but each time I was saved by a miracle because God was with me. My dearest wish that I articulated in my two books and several talks was that women be granted the vote and have the right to be elected, and it was realized."

"Should women participate in political life?" Nuwayhid asked.

"Women are perfectly suited to such activity because it requires flexibility, competence, decorum, candor, self-sacrifice, justice, and prosperity for all; these are qualities women practice in their little kingdom, in the home and with the family. They run the household, a kind of mini-parliament. They set laws and rules that require great understanding, wisdom, and sensitivity to their role as keeper of the peace. There are many examples of women's success in the field of politics. Let's look, for example, at the beginning of Islam when Khadija, Mother of the Faithful, was the wise counselor of her husband, the Prophet (peace be upon him), and she helped him a great deal in diffusing his message. Throughout world history there have been women who have proven how successful women can be in politics. Take, for example, Cleopatra, Zanubiya, Queen Victoria, Indira Gandhi and others. Although the case of Lebanon is more limited we need to mention Princess Habus Arslan and Nazira Jumblat." She ended the interview optimistically: "Now women have achieved political freedom and equal rights and duties with men and they are qualified to occupy the highest positions because of their intellect, maturity, work and balance" (Nuwayhid, 1986, pp. 94–99).

On 18 January 1974, eighteen months later, Nazira gave a very different interview with the surprising title "Political Parties Corrupt Women." A little over a year before the outbreak of the civil war (1975–1990), Sa'd Sami Ramadan from *Al-Hasna'* introduced Nazira as the brave pioneer of a movement to liberate women from their outworn chains. Almost fifty years earlier, he wrote, her feminist challenge had sparked a battle that was fought on the pages of newspapers and magazines and in clubs and that she finally won.

"Where is she now? She lives in a spacious, old house decorated in oriental style where she spends day and much of the night reading, an occupation that she considers to be the best nourishment in the autumn of life. In this small world of hers that is filled with memories of glory and emancipatory and educational movements for women, she posed the first question: 'What reminded you of me? I live here far from the limelight or any activity worth mentioning. Thank you for what you are doing and for this visit that revives images from the distant past when I worked for the liberation of Arab women.'"

She went on to talk about the strides women had made since that time even while decrying the current overemphasis on women's work. Surely, women in need or those who had time should have every opportunity to work, but the demand for employment in all spheres of life was what she called a "fashion" with which she disagreed. Although men and women were equally capable of working, there were limits. "Eastern women" should abide by tradition and local customs. Young women should not be allowed to go out in the evenings and to come home whenever they wanted. Affluent women should not leave their children in the care of servants and thus threaten the integrity and health of the family. She went so far as to say that the contested Qur'anic verse about men's superiority to women was right. Yet, in all of this reactionary discourse there was still a trace of the fiery woman she had once been. She recalled her disappointment in not being able to train to be a doctor. Still conversant with the scriptures she had mastered when she was a teenager, she cited Traditions to prove that it was God's will that women vote, but that they should not participate in politics that corrupt women's basic feminine nature. No, she told Ramadan in closing, she was not going to write anything else because of her poor health. During an intestinal operation at Hotel Dieu, the surgeons discovered that she had cancer.

Later that year she moved with Shafiq and Amin to an apartment Nabil had bought the previous year in Mar Taala. It was too dangerous to stay in Ras al-Naba where Sunni militiamen were gathering strength and the Palestinian leadership was becoming entrenched. After Black September, the 1970 military operation of the Jordanian King Hussein against Palestinian militants, Yasser Arafat and a large number of his followers decamped to Beirut where their military presence exacerbated simmering tensions.

During the first two years of the war, international communications became increasingly difficult, and in late 1976 there were virtually none. When Nabil finally succeeded in getting through, Amin picked up the phone. After a brief exchange, he asked to speak with Maman. There was absolute silence, and he knew she had gone. She had died on 2 December 1976 at the Sacre Coeur Hospital in Yarze, a suburb of Beirut. She ended her life in the arms of nuns and under the protection of her beloved Santa Rita, the patron saint of impossible or lost causes.

Immediately after she died there was a crisis about how to bury her. The war was raging in that area and Shafiq called the Phalange militia leadership for help getting the body up the mountain to Baaqline. They agreed to take her body out of the Christian quarter where she had died and over which they had control. Calling for a one-hour ceasefire, they took her to the Druze barricade. There they handed the corpse over to Jumblat's militias that were under the command of her brother Kamil.

Shafiq and Amin left Mar Taala that had become too hot for Druze inhabitants, and some Maronites occupied the apartment. They moved to the family home in Baaqline. After the Syrian invasion of 1976, the Druze situation became dire. In March 1977, Kamal Jumblat – leader of the Lebanese Druzes and founder of the secular Progressive Socialist Party – was assassinated, and a few days later his sister Linda al-Atrash, Nina's mother, was also killed. By that time, Shafiq's fortunes had dwindled to almost nothing and he summoned his sons to apologize: "I did not leave you material goods, but I did leave you a good name"– and the huge house in Baaqline where he died on 17 August 1978 at age 86.

Nazira had been buried in the al-Halabi cemetery close to the historical cemetery of Baaqline. Shafiq, however, was not buried with his wife because, strangely enough, there was no room in the al-Halabi vault. Instead he was interred in the Hamade cemetery because his mother had been a Hamadeh.

Amin was in charge of the arrangements for the condolences for both parents. Crowds of people came from Ayn Qani to the Baaqline meetinghouse where the dead lie in state. Unlike Sunni and Shiite Muslims, Druzes are not wrapped in a shroud. Like Christians, they lie in state dressed in their best clothes. For both funerals, the women mourners gathered in a room, sitting around the open coffin sipping black, unsweetened coffee and wailing. Then the men came to close the coffin and take it into the men's quarters. After reciting prayers for the dead out of the Druze "Book of Wisdom," the *mashayikh* proceeded out of the house leading the coffin down the main street until they came to the cemetery. Although the funerals were held in Baaqline, the people who attended were from Ayn Qani. They were the ones who carried the coffins aloft, each one jostling for the honor of being pallbearer.

Why was it not the people of Baaqline who carried the coffins? Nabil explained that his father had offended local sensibilities. Although he was far from being an observant Druze, the community had once proposed to make Shafiq *Shaykh Aql*, the highest spiritual position in the hierarchy. He had refused on intellectual grounds because he despised Druze rituals, especially those connected with death, and had rarely if ever attended the condolence ceremonies.

Druze tomb in Baaqline

Funerals, however, are of paramount importance to the Druzes, perhaps because they believe that the soul of the person transmigrates into the body of a newborn babe. The condolences are thus also an occasion to celebrate a reincarnation. It may be acceptable to miss a wedding; it is inexcusable to miss a funeral (El Halabi, 2005, p. 103). So, tit for tat!

After his parents' death, Amin took care of his aunt Munira who continued to teach in a primary school. Samia Saab recalled the day he asked her to come with him: "I was shocked to find Munira living in abject poverty. She had put on a lot of weight. She was sad and as always silent." She cowered alone in her single room throughout the civil war and became known among the local militiamen who made a sport of terrifying her. She died in 1988.

His two brothers still in Rome, Amin was left in charge of the house. His schizophrenia was far advanced, exacerbated by the loss of his parents and the chaos and violence in the country. He could not protect the contents of the house, especially after the Syrians invaded in the summer of 1976. They stripped it of its contents. During the seventeen years following his father's death, Amin divided his time between Baaqline where he lived alone and Rome where he spent several months each year with his brothers.

He died in 1994. Like his grandfather, he prepared for his death carefully. He pulled a rocking chair up to a window on the ground floor of the Baaqline house in full view of passersby and, covering himself with a blanket, he awaited death. The terrible loneliness of his life in this town where the family was so marginalized is etched in this story. Fawzi, the loyal driver, who had kept an eye on him, found him cold in the chair.

CONCLUSION

The first woman to write an entire book on Muslim women's rights and absolute equality, the young Nazira Zeineddine bridged two stages in the development of Islamic feminist thought. She connects the pro-women writings of Egyptian and Syrian reformists at the end of the nineteenth century with those of Muslim women everywhere who are concerned with the misogyny and growing control of Islamists at the end of the twentieth century. Although her arguments against the veil reflected current thinking on the subject, her interpretations of certain Qur'anic verses that empower women and release them from concocted constraints were remarkable for the era in which she was writing. It is above all her questioning of the soundness of the Tradition denigrating women's intellect and religion, included in the canonical compilations of Traditions by Muslim and Bukhari, that mark the radical nature of her polemic. It is here that her work can be seen to depart from the pro-women, anti-veiling hermeneutics of Muhammad Abduh and Qasim Amin and to anticipate the dissection of orthodox texts conducted by Islamic feminists like the Moroccan Fatima Mernissi during the 1990s. Her *ijtihad* of the notorious Tradition was ground-breaking, but it fell on to stony ground. There was no network of pro-women religious activists who could pick up the argument, circulate it, and develop its implications. By placing Nazira Zeineddine in a chain of Sharia-minded intellectuals I propose that she provides a missing link connecting two *fin de siècle* moments in the history Islamic feminism.

How was this call for freedom of religions, of knowledge, of will, and of the liberation of women and of nationalist self-assertion silenced? "The Girl," who had compelled serious attention to misogyn-ist readings of Islamic scriptures, infuriated the shaykhs in the late

1920s, and driven a wedge into her society, had fallen through the cracks of history. Caught in the decline and fall of two bourgeois families, her biography skirts the edge of modern Lebanese history from the end of the Ottoman Empire through the French Mandate, independence, and the civil war.

At a time when women were expected to be quiet and invisible, Nazira had spoken without fear. She had felt protected and encouraged by her father. Even when one of the most powerful shaykhs of the day attacked her and wrote an entire book to refute her, she was not cowed. Soon, however, she stopped writing and disappeared.

Did her Druze identity play a role in her eclipse? By the mid-1930s, the Druzes' historical dominance in Mount Lebanon had been undermined. Whereas the Ottomans had relied on the Druze feudal structure to govern indirectly, the French favored the Christians and especially their long-time protégés, the Maronites (Joumblatt1978, pp. 72–76). The establishment in 1932 of the confessional system of political representation that parceled out positions according to religious affiliation favored the Maronites and disenfranchised the Druzes. Religious differences mattered more and more at a time when the Sunni hierarchy was insisting on rigid notions of Islamic orthodoxy. The Druzes were no longer considered simply Muslims but rather members of a heterodox religious sect. Even though critics rarely mentioned Nazira's Druze identity, it may have played a role in the suppression of her books.

But as I have demonstrated, Nazira did contribute to this marginalization. Her reckless challenge to the religious authorities of the day may have united them against her and her books. Moreover, she seems to have lost the taste for the fight after publishing *The Girl and the Shaykhs*. Her marriage to a man of the state who would not tolerate his wife's visibility was the *coup de grâce*. Her last interview, given four years before her death, indicated that this woman, who had struggled to make a case for women's equality in all spheres, no longer believed in women's rights to political participation. The transformation between the girl and the woman was so profound that it was almost as though they were two different people. Did the woman betray the girl? I do not believe that she did.

Although more extreme than most, the gap between the two ages of this woman is instructive when we think about the construction and development of the self over time. Not every act describes and shapes a corresponding identity. The first book, *Unveiling and Veiling,* was written from a contingent speaking position and at a particular juncture in the history of modern Arab feminism. Nazira was not creating a dissident identity through her writings. During a decade when religious conservatives and feminists were at loggerheads, she was attacking and trying to stop the shaykhs from depriving women of their most basic rights. By the 1930s, however, many shaykhs in Syria and Lebanon had reduced the debate around the veil to a simple binary: those who supported veiling were good Muslims, those who opposed were not only bad Muslims but were also subject to the accusation that they were collaborators with the French.

Why should Nazira stay true to that moment? She had reacted responsibly, if impetuously at the time of a perceived injury to women. However, when she became the wife of a politician with a volatile career and the mother of three sons she no longer seemed to have felt free to express the kind of opinion available to her in an earlier existence.

In piecing together Nazira's story, I have tried to make sense of her struggle to balance commitments to family, women, and society. I have traced her changing understanding of her self from empowered and outraged public intellectual to silenced wife and mother. Education had played a vital role in her life. She had attended the best girls' schools in 1920s Lebanon and her husband had studied in Paris and then briefly served as minister of education under the French. It was unthinkable that the boys' education should be compromised.

Interest in Nazira and her writings has vacillated over the past eighty years; the most recent stage began in the late 1980s when Islamic feminism was on the rise and scholars concerned with women's rights in Islam discovered her. Unlike Huda Shaarawi, known primarily for her one emblematic act of unveiling in Cairo station and almost not at all for her writings, Nazira has until recently been known only through her two books that have never been translated out of their formal, high Arabic.

A mark of how relevant but also neglected her books had become can be seen in others' use of her title, *Unveiling and Veiling*, without acknowledgment. In 1982, Safinaz Qazim could publish her pamphlet *Fi mas'alat al-sufur wa al-hijab* (On the Question of Unveiling and Veiling) that deals with some of the issues found in Nazira's text without a single reference to the author of the original text of that title. Kariman Hamza entitled her autobiography *Rihlati min al-sufur ila al-hijab* (My Journey from Unveiling to Veiling), also without attribution. Was the lack of reference in these cases deliberate or due to ignorance?

In the past decade things have changed. A mark of the new and generalized interest in Nazira and her first book came on 27 January 2010. The winner of the MBC-TV *Jeopardy* contest was Cleopatra Iskini, a Lebanese taxi driver who was asked: "Who is the author of *Al-sufur wa al-hijab*, a book that caused a furor in its day?" A quick consultation with the permitted counsel came up with the answer: Nazira Zeineddine. The 150,000 Saudi riyals were hers!

GLOSSARY

'Aql reason or intellect

Burqa' face veil and all-enveloping garment worn primarily in Central Asia

Chouf mountain range southeast of Beirut

Hajj annual pilgrimage to Mecca

Hanafi one of four Sunni schools of law

Ijtihad personal reasoning based on the principal sources of the Islamic tradition the Qur'an and the Traditions

Jahiliya Pre-Islamic era

Jiddu term of endearment for Grandfather

Jihad struggle that may be spiritual or military

Kaaba sacred shrine in Mecca toward which Muslims turn for the five daily prayers

Madrasa school

Mashayikh Druze elders

Mufti interpreter of Islamic law

Muharram a month in the Islamic calendar; on the tenth of the month Shiites lament the murder of Husayn, the grandson of the Prophet Muhammad

Mujahida woman participating in *jihad*

Mujtahida woman practitioner of *ijtihad*

Musattaha Druze woman with white cloth drawn over nose and mouth

Niqab face veil

Shaykh authority on Islam

Sufur unveiling

Sunna the sayings and doings of the Prophet Muhammad that became legally binding precedents

Tafsir commentary on the Qur'an

Traditions words and actions of the Prophet reported by his
    Companions

Ulama scholars of Islamic texts

Umma worldwide community of Muslims

'Umra minor pilgrimage to Mecca

Wafd delegation

WORKS CITED

Ahmed, Leila. 1992. *Women and Gender in Islam*. New Haven: Yale
    University Press

Asad, Talal. 1986. *The Idea of an Anthropology of Islam*. Washington DC:
    Georgetown University Press

Badran, Margot and cooke, miriam. 1990. *Opening the Gates. A Century of
    Arab Feminist Writing*. Bloomington, Indiana: Indiana University Press
    (2nd edn 2004)

Baron, Beth. 2005. *Egypt as a Woman: Nationalism, Gender and Politics*.
    Berkeley: University of California Press

Booth, Marilyn. 2001. *May her Likes be Multiplied: Biography and Gender
    Politics in Egypt*. Berkeley: University of California Press

Bu Matar, Nabil. 2008. *Nazira Zeineddine ra'ida fi al-taharrur al-niswi*
    (Nazira Zeineddine: Pioneer of Women's Liberation). Chouf: Al-Dar
    al-Taqaddumiya

Cuinet, Vital. 1891. *La Turquie d'Asie. Géographie Administrative*. Paris:
    Ernest Leroux, vol. II

Fawwaz, Zaynab. 1895. *Al-durr al-manthur fi tabaqat rabbat al-khudur*
    (Pearls scattered in women's quarters). Beirut

al-Ghalayini, Mustafa. 1908. *Al-Islam Ruh al-Madaniya aw al-din al-Islami
    wa al-Lurd Krumir* (Islam Spirit of Civilization; or the Islamic Religion
    and Lord Cromer). Beirut: Quzma

———. 1928. *Nazarat fi "Al-sufur wa al-hijab"* (Views on the Book
    "Unveiling and Veiling"). Beirut: Quzma

El Halabi, Abbas. 2005. *Les Druzes: Vivre avec l'avenir*. Beirut: Dar an-Nahar

Hirschberg, H. Z. 1969. "The Druzes" in A. J. Arberry, *Religion in the
    Middle East,* volume 2. London: Cambridge University Press

Hitti, Philip. 1928. *The Origins of the Druze People and Religion*. New York:
    Columbia University Press

al-Jawhari, Aida. 2007. *Ramziyat al-hijab: mafahim wa dalalat* (Symbolism
    of the Veil: Concepts and Meanings). Beirut: Markaz Dirasat al-Wahda
    al-'Arabiya

Joumblatt, Kamal. 1978. *Pour le Liban*. Paris: Editions Stock

Khalaf, Samir. 1979. *Persistence and Change in Nineteenth-Century Lebanon: a Sociological Essay*. Beirut: AUB Press

Kurzman, Charles. 1998. *Liberal Islam. A Sourcebook*. Oxford: Oxford University Press

——— 2002. *Modernist Islam 1840–1940*. Oxford: Oxford University Press

"*lamha 'an Shafiq al-Halabi wa haramihi*" (A Note about Shafiq al-Halabi and his Wife). *Al-Amani* (1980), #134–135

Lubnan hayat rajul safha khalida fi sudur al-nas (Lebanon: The life of a man, an eternal page in the hearts of people). Matba'a Anjilik: Beirut

McCann, Graham. 1991. "Biographical Boundaries: Sociology and Marilyn Monroe" in Mike Featherstone et al., eds, *The Body: Social Process and Cultural Theory*. London: Sage Publications

Mill, John Stuart. 1869. *The Subjection of Women* (www.constitution.org/jsm/women.htm accessed 17.4.2007)

Nuwayhid, Nadia al-Jurdi. 1986. *Nisa' min biladi* (Women from my Country). Beirut: al-Mu'assasa al-'Arabiya lil-Dirasat wa al-Nashr

Qurtas, Wadad al-Maqdisi. 1982. *Dhikrayat, 1917–1977* (Memoirs 1917–1977). Beirut: Mu'assasat al-Abhath al-'Arabiya

Ramadan, Sa'd Sami. 1974. "*Ahzab siyasiya tufsid al-nisa'*" (Political parties corrupt women). Interview with Nazira Zeineddine in *Al-Hasna' (18 Jan. 1974), #645*

Schulze, Reinhard. 2000 (1995). *A Modern History of the Islamic World* (tr. Azizeh Azodi). London: I.B. Tauris

Shaaban, Bouthaina. 1993. "The Hidden History of Arab Feminism" in *Ms. Magazine* (May/June)

Tannous, Afif I. 2004. *Village Roots and Beyond*. Beirut: Dar Nelson

Tarabulsi, Fawwaz. 2008. *Tarikh Lubnan al-hadith min al-imara ila ittifaq al-Taif* (The History of Modern Lebanon from Princedom until the Taif Agreement). Beirut: Riyad al-Rayyes Books

Thompson, Elizabeth. 2000. *Colonial Citizens. Republican Rights, Paternal Privilege, and Gender in French Syria and Lebanon*. New York: Columbia University Press

Yarid, Nazik Saba. 2001. "*Nazira Zayn al-Din 1908–1976 bayna al-tahaddi wa al-iltizam*" (Nazira Zeineddine 1908–1976 between challenge and commitment). *Bahithat* special issue: "Arab Women in the 1920s", pp. 243–261

Zachs, Fruma & Halevi, Sharon. 2009. "From Difa' al-Nisa' to Mas'alat al-Nisa' in Greater Syria." *International Journal of Middle East Studies* 41/4

Zeineddine, Nazira. 1998 (1928). *Al-sufur wa al-hijab. Muhadarat wa nazarat fi tahrir al-mar'a wa al-tajaddud al-ijtima'i fi al-'alam al-islami* (Unveiling and Veiling. Lectures and Views concerning the Liberation of Women and Social Renewal in the Islamic World). Introduction by Bouthaina Shaaban. Damascus: Dar al-Mada

———. 1998 (1929). *Al-fatat wa al-shuyukh. Nazarat wa munazarat fi al-sufur wa al-hijab wa tahrir al-'aql wa tahrir al-mar'a wa al-tajaddud al-ijtima'i fi al-'alam al-islami* (The Girl and the Shaykhs. Views and Debates about "Unveiling and Veiling" and the Liberation of the Intellect and the Liberation of Women and Social Renewal in the Islamic World). Damascus: Dar al-Mada

———. 1932. "Kitab maftuh ila al-ustadh al-Ghalayini" (Open Letter to Mr. al-Ghalayini). *Al-Nida'*, 25 June

———. 1932 "Al-sufur wa al-hijab" (Unveiling and Veiling). *Al-Farfur* #47, 2 October

INDEX

Abas, Said, 48
'Abd al-Rahman al-Huss, 97
'Abduh, Muhammad, 37, 54, 129
al-'Abid Bayhum, Nazik, 9, 31, 105
Abu Hanifa, 60, 89
Abu Rashid, Salima, 6
Afernuh, Alexandra, 6
al-Afghani, Jamal al-Din, 37, 83
Ahliya School, 30–1
Ahmad, Labiba, 8
Aisha, Wife of the Prophet, 42, 59, 84–5
'Alayini, 'Abdallah, 48
'Ali, the Prophet's cousin, 88
'Aliya, Iqbal, 105
American University, 31–2
Amin, Qasim, 5–6, 11, 37, 46, 54, 55, 70,
    88, 123, 129; New Woman, The, 88
'aql, 37–8
Arab Academy, 121
Arab Literary Association, 45–6
Arab Women Workers' Union, 105
Arab Women's Conference, 111
Arafat, Yasser, 125
Arslan, Habus, 124
Asad, Talal, 91
'Atallah, Marie Yani, 6
Ataturk, 47, 54, 62
al-Atrash, Asmahan, 26, 26, 107
al-Atrash, Emir Hasan, 25–6
al-Atrash, Nina, 26
al-Atrash, Pasha, 25
Ayn Qani, 19; region, 17, 20; terrace, 22;
    Zeineddine Mansion, xii
Azhar, 89
al-Azhari, Ahmad Muhyi al-Din, 48

Baaqline: al-Halabi Mansion, xiii; Druze
    tomb, 127
al-Badiya, Bahithat, 7
al-Baghdadi, Said, 48

al-Baidawi, Nasir al-Din, 59
Balfour Declaration, 25, 113
al-Banna, Hasan, 47
al-Baraqi, Muhammad b. Yaqub, 88
Beirut, 20, 121
Bey, Ahmad Nami, 60, 97
Bey, Ihsan Haqqi, 105
bint Muzahim, Assia, 42
Booth, Marilyn, 7
Bu Matar, Nabil, 76–7, 96, 120
al-Bukhari, Abu 'Abdallah, 33–4, 88, 129
al-Bustani, Butrus, 3

Chamoun, Camille, 119
Chamoun, Zelfa, 119
Cleopatra, 124
confessionalism, 104–5, 130
Constitutional Bloc see National Bloc
Cromer, Lord, 6

debate: use of, 91
Deoband, 89
Dimashqiya, Julia Tu'ma, 6, 30
Druze, the: division from Muslims, 24; a
    minority, 104–5; women, 56
Druze tomb, Baaqline, 127

Edde, Emil, 108, 113
Edirne, 16
Edivar, Khalida Adib, 10
education: secularization of, 13–14
El Halabi, Abbas, 26–7, 37–8

Fakhuri, Jamil, 38, 44–5, 109
al-Faqih, Yusuf, 45, 63, 90
Fawwaz, Zaynab, 5, 57–8
feminist post-colonial theory, 82
France: Mandate in Lebanon, 24–7, 104;
    Mandate in Syria, 24; see also French, the
Freij, Alexandra de, 106

Freij, Alice Shiha de, 106
French, the: example of, 97–8, 99;
    Zeineddine family loyalty to, 104,
    110–11
Fu'ad, King, 79; "The Voice of Truth",
    64–5, 65

Gandhi, Indira, 124
Gaulle, Charles de, xiv; residence in
    Karakol Druze, xiv
gender politics, 7
al-Ghalayini, Mustafa, 39–44, 48, 52, 57,
    80–2, 83–4, 87, 92, 94, 95, 96, 97;
    Views on the Book "Attributed to Miss Nazira
    Zeineddine", 69–77
al-Ghazali, 33, 37
Girl and the Shaykhs, The (Zeineddine),
    77–85; rebuttal of criticism, 87–93;
    review of, 78

Hafiz, Ibrahim, 46
al-Halabi, Amin, 107, 109, 120, 122,
    125–8
al-Halabi, Arij, 109, 110, 112, 117
al-Halabi, Fedwa, 114
al-Halabi Mansion, Baaqline, xiii
al-Halabi, Naayim, 114
al-Halabi, Nabil, 109, 112, 113, 114–15,
    121–2, 123, 125, 127
al-Halabi, Shafiq, 22, 106–15, 119–20,
    125–6, 132; death, 126–8; governor of
    Beirut, 109–11; political career, 108,
    113, 114–15, 119
Hamdan, Salim, 48, 80, 89–90
Hamza, Kariman, 132
al-Hasani, Taj al-Din, 60; letter to Nazira,
    61
Hashim, Labiba, 6
al-Hurr al-'Amili, Muhammad b. Hasan,
    88
Hussein, King, 125

ibn Hajar, al-Shihab, 34
Ibn Hanbal, 114
ibn Qays al-Hilali, Salim, 88
Iskini, Cleopatra, 132

al-Jabi, Said, 48, 80, 88

al-Jawhari, Aida, xii
Jewish state, establishment of, 25, 113
Joan of Arc: as model, 7, 64–5, 79
Jumblat, Kamal, 104, 126
Jumblat, Linda, 26
Jumblat, Nazira, 107, 124
Jumblat, Sami Bey, 48
al-Jurdi Nuwayhid, Nadia, 123
juyub: interpretation of, 92–3

Kandiyani, Mademoiselle, 94
Karakol Druze: de Gaulle's residence, xiv;
    guests at, 29
Khadija, Mother of the Faithful, 42, 59,
    124
al-Khatib, Zeineddine Pasha Hasan,
    13–14, 14
al-Khuri, Bishara, 107–8, 111, 114
al-Khuri, Rashid, 95–6
King-Crane Commission, 25
Kirik Killiesi, 15–16
al-Kirmani, 'Abd al-Qadir, 48
Kozan, Anatolia, 15
Kurd, Muhammad Bey, 61
Kurzman, Charles, 91

Lebanese Women's Union, 31
Lebanon: 1932 census, 104; under French
    administration, 24–7, 104
"Legality of the Veil", 66–7
Liberation of Women (Amin), 6, 70, 72, 88
Lycée Français Laique, 32

al-Maghribi, 'Abd al-Qadir, 60–1
al-Majdub, Ibrahim, 48–9
Maronites, 104, 130
Mary, the Virgin, 42, 46
Mernissi, Fatima, 129
Mill, John Stuart, 4, 40, 82, 98–9
missionaries: alleged influence of, 70,
    81–3, 88–9
Mufti, the, 66–7, 79
Muhammad, the Prophet, 37, 40, 88;
    Companions of, 32–3
Musa, Nabawiya, 9
musattaha, 56
Muslim Brothers, 47
Muslim ibn al-Hajjaj, 33–4, 129

Mutran, Khalil Bey, 96

Naja, Muhammad 'Umar, 48–9
Najaf, 89
Naqqash, Alfred, 108, 112
al-Nasfi, Abdullah bin Ahmad bin
    Mahmud, 59, 92
al-Nasfi, Hafidh al-Din, 56
Nasif, Malik Hifni, 48
National Bloc, 108, 113, 119
Nawfal, Hind, 6
*Nazira Zeineddine: Pioneer of Women's
    Liberation* (Nabil and Hayat Bu Matar),
    xiii–xiv
New Islamic Woman, the, 8
New Woman, the, 8

Organization of the Syrian Union, 121
Ottomans, the, 19, 21
Oxford University, 89

Pasha, Jamal, 19, 21–2, 23–4, 108
polygyny, 26, 36, 41, 53–4
Ponsot, Henri, 73–4, 97

qarna, 58–9
al-Qayati al-Azhari, Muhammad Ibrahim,
    48, 54–5
Qazim, Safinaz, 131–2
al-Qummi, 'Ali Babawayh, 88
Qur'an: clothing in, 51–2; women in,
    36–7; women's roles, 58–60
Qurtas, Wadad al-Maqdisi, 25, 30–1,
    109

Ramadan, Sa'd Sami, 124
al-Raziq, 'Ali 'Abd, 61–2
repudiation, 37
al-Rifai, Fawzi, 62
al-Rihani, Amin, 96
al-Rusafi, Ma'ruf, 77

Saab, Afifa, 6
Saab, Nabila, xiv
Saab, Najla, xiv, 111
Saab, Raja, 103
Saab, Samia, xiv, 22–3, 37, 103, 111, 115,
    128

Saadiya Saad al-Din, 6
Salam, 'Anbara, 45
Scattered Pearls, 57–8
Shaaban, Bouthaina, 6
al-Shaar, Hala *see* Zeineddine, Hala
Shaarawi, Huda, 9, 63, 111, 131
al-Shamitili, Mahmud, 48
Shishakli, Adib, 113
Shumayyil, Shibli, 80
Stanton, Elizabeth Cady, 4
Subjection of Women, The, 98–9
al-Sufi al-Khazin, 'Ala al-Din, 59
al-Suhl, Taqi al-Din, 45–6
Sykes-Picot Agreement, 24

Taqieddine, Ambassador, 122
al-Tarabulsi, Mustafa Rahim, 48, 51–2
Taylor, Harriet, 98–9
al-Taymuriya, Aisha, 4–5, 55
Thompson, Elizabeth, 96
Tradition, the, 32–6, 129; Nazira on, 53;
    and veiling, 52; women in, 35

'Umar, caliph, 56
UNESCO, 111
unveiling, 94–5; defense of, 90;
    definition, 89
Unveiling and Veiling (Zeineddine), 3,
    10–11, 131; alleged influence of
    missionaries on, 70, 81–3, 88–9;
    authorship disputed, 93–4; Christian
    praise for, 95–6; *ijtihad*, 91; language,
    90–3; reception of, 60; significance of,
    123; themes of freedom and equality,
    51–60, 99; transcendental authority,
    97; use of, by other writers, 131–2; use
    of scripture, 96

veil, the, 42–3; attitudes to, 10–11; a civil
    matter, 97; as corrupting, 52; debate
    about, 3, 131; and immoral behavior,
    54; no mandate for, 45–9; original
    purpose, 56, 57; protests against, 7–8;
    significance of, 4–6, 39–40; in the
    Tradition, 52; undermining society,
    54–5; and women's rights, 9; *see also*
    unveiling
Victoria, Queen, 124

Wollstonecraft, Mary, 4
women: biography of, 6–7; Druze, 56;
    equal rights of, 36–8; feminist post-
    colonial theory, 82; freedom and
    equality, 51–4; leaders of Islam, 57–8;
    the New Islamic Woman, 8; the New
    Woman, 8; in the Qur'an, 36–7,
    58–60; reason, 54, 55; religion, 55–7;
    rights of, 9, 123; roles of, 124–5;
    suffrage, 104; supporters of prophets,
    42; in the Tradition, 35; unveiled,
    94–5; value to society, 7; and the veil, 9
women's witness, 37, 62

al-Yaziji, Warda, 9–10, 93
Young Turks, 18

Zaghlul, Sa'd, 6, 7–8
Zaghlul, Safiyya, 8, 132
al-Zahawi, Jamil Sidqi, 77
al-Zahra, Fatima, 42, 57
al-Zaim, Husni, 113
al-Zaim, Salah al-Din, 48, 80, 88
Zanubiya, 124
Zaynab, 23, 56, 114, 116
Zeineddine, Amira, 22, 23–4, 56, 103
Zeineddine, Arij, xv
Zeineddine, Hala, 18–19, 22, 70, 75, 76,
    103, 116
Zeineddine, Kamil, 22, 104, 113, 116,
    117–18, 126
Zeineddine Mansion, Ayn Qani, xii
Zeineddine, Monique Eugene, 116
Zeineddine, Muhammad, 14, 22, 23–4
Zeineddine, Munir, 19, 69, 70, 71, 104,
    116, 117

Zeineddine, Munira, 19, 23, 29–31, 30,
    70, 103, 116, 117, 128
Zeineddine, Nabil, xv
Zeineddine, Najla, 22
Zeineddine, Nazira, 26, 29, 30, 110, 117;
    "An Open Letter to Mr. al-Ghalayini",
    105; birth of, 18; challenge to religious
    authorities, 130; compared to Joan of
    Arc, 64–5, 79; death, 125–8; Druze
    identity, 130; education, 4–5, 23,
    29–32, 62–3, 94–5, 132; eulogy for
    Iqbal 'Aliya, 105; married life, 106–15,
    119–20, 123, 124–5; motherhood,
    121–2; "Oh East", 105; place in Islamic
    feminist thought, 129–30, 131;
    "Political Parties Corrupt Women",
    124–5; public lectures, 44–6; public
    life, disappearance from, 129–32;
    public life, return to, 123–5; social
    work, 120; study of the Qur'an, 36–7;
    study of the Tradition, 32–6; "The Girl
    and the Shaykhs on Unveiling and
    veiling", 90; "Two Ills in Arab Society",
    105; on the veil, 9; "Why I prefer
    unveiling to veiling", 45–6; wish to
    become doctor, 31; see also Girl and the
    Shaykhs, The; Unveiling and Veiling
Zeineddine, Said, xiii–xiv, 116–17, 117,
    118
Zeineddine, Said Bey, xii, xiv–xv, 13–19,
    15, 16, 22–3, 48–9, 56, 60, 62, 99,
    103, 108, 111; on al-Ghalayini, 39–40,
    43–4; death, 115–16; reading of al-
    Ghalayini's book, 69–77; retirement,
    113–14; teaches Nazira scripture, 32–7
Ziyada, Mayy, 8, 9–10, 31, 48, 93